Cambridge Elements

Elements in Evolutionary Economics
edited by
John Foster
University of Queensland
Jason Potts
RMIT University
Isabel Almudi
University of Zaragoza
Francisco Fatas-Villafranca
University of Zaragoza
David A. Harper
New York University

INSTITUTIONAL ACCELERATION

The Consequences of Technological Change in a Digital Economy

Darcy W. E. Allen
RMIT University

Chris Berg
RMIT University

Jason Potts
RMIT University

Shaftesbury Road, Cambridge CB2 8EA, United Kingdom

One Liberty Plaza, 20th Floor, New York, NY 10006, USA

477 Williamstown Road, Port Melbourne, VIC 3207, Australia

314–321, 3rd Floor, Plot 3, Splendor Forum, Jasola District Centre, New Delhi – 110025, India

103 Penang Road, #05–06/07, Visioncrest Commercial, Singapore 238467

Cambridge University Press is part of Cambridge University Press & Assessment, a department of the University of Cambridge.

We share the University's mission to contribute to society through the pursuit of education, learning and research at the highest international levels of excellence.

www.cambridge.org
Information on this title: www.cambridge.org/9781009638630

DOI: 10.1017/9781009638616

© Darcy W. E. Allen, Chris Berg and Jason Potts 2025

This publication is in copyright. Subject to statutory exception and to the provisions of relevant collective licensing agreements, no reproduction of any part may take place without the written permission of Cambridge University Press & Assessment.

When citing this work, please include a reference to the DOI 10.1017/9781009638616

First published 2025

A catalogue record for this publication is available from the British Library

ISBN 978-1-009-63863-0 Hardback
ISBN 978-1-009-63860-9 Paperback
ISSN 2514-3573 (online)
ISSN 2514-3581 (print)

Cambridge University Press & Assessment has no responsibility for the persistence or accuracy of URLs for external or third-party internet websites referred to in this publication and does not guarantee that any content on such websites is, or will remain, accurate or appropriate.

For EU product safety concerns, contact us at Calle de José Abascal, 56, 1°, 28003 Madrid, Spain, or email eugpsr@cambridge.org

Institutional Acceleration

The Consequences of Technological Change in a Digital Economy

Elements in Evolutionary Economics

DOI: 10.1017/9781009638616
First published online: May 2025

Darcy W. E. Allen
RMIT University

Chris Berg
RMIT University

Jason Potts
RMIT University

Author for correspondence: Darcy W. E. Allen, darcy.allen@rmit.edu.au

Abstract: This Element develops a theory of institutional acceleration to explain the transformation to a digital economy through a cluster of frontier technologies: artificial intelligence, blockchain, quantum computing, cryptography, and low earth orbit infrastructure. Unlike previous technological revolutions, these technologies transform not how we organise things, but how we coordinate economic activity. The authors' supertransition thesis explains why these digital technologies shouldn't be understood in isolation, but rather should be understood in how they combine to create new institutional possibilities, leading to more open, complex, and global economic systems. Drawing on evolutionary economics and institutional theory, this Element shows how this evolutionary process is reshaping our institutional economic architecture. Ultimately, institutional acceleration drives greater computation and knowledge into our economic systems.

Keywords: institutional evolution, supertransition, institutional technology, digital economy, technological change

© Darcy W. E. Allen, Chris Berg and Jason Potts 2025

ISBNs: 9781009638630 (HB), 9781009638609 (PB), 9781009638616 (OC)
ISSNs: 2514-3573 (online), 2514-3581 (print)

Contents

Introduction	1
1 The Supertransition Thesis	2
2 Vectors of Technological Change	10
3 Combinatorial Innovation and the Supertransition	20
4 Institutional Acceleration	37
5 An Economy of Digital Institutions	47
6 Adaptation and Agency in the Supertransition	57
7 i/acc	65
References	69

Introduction

Like speakers, some books need no introduction. This Element does, because we have written for three very different readers. So let us make separate briefings now before we all head out together.

To our colleagues – the evolutionary, innovation and institutional economists, those concerned with deep economic dynamics, and those who we consider to be our intellectual community – we offer this Element as a statement of a new approach that explores technological innovation and institutional evolution as a unified process. This is in the combinatorial tradition of technological dynamics (à la Brian Arthur, Stuart Kauffman, et al.) and somewhat against the Schumpeterian tradition of innovation trajectories as the unit of analysis. For you, we offer an outline of a new evolutionary economics for a digital economy.

To our colleagues across the business schools and social sciences, we offer a new social science method to analyse consequences of technological dynamics. This Element builds on our earlier work using institutional economics – which we previously applied to a particular technology (blockchain) – to explain the future with a new way of theorising technology by forecasting institutions. In business schools and social science today we treat technological and institutional dynamics as mostly separate phenomena. Until recently, this has been a reasonable assumption. Yet with digital technologies as institutional technologies – that is, hard tech for coordinating people (e.g. internet, smart contracts) – that clean separation no longer holds. And so we are in a new world, and require a new framework. This Element presents a new way to study deeply disruptive large-scale changes in the economy and society as they occur by forecasting technology-driven institutional dynamics. Research in this genre looks different from traditional business school and social science research, but we cannot let dogmatic adherence to past methods prevent us from describing how the world is changing around us.

And to those working with tech in the real world – the industry leaders and entrepreneurs and investors who are building, creating, and betting on the future, as well as regulators and policymakers who are trying to understand your role as the old models of politics and economics shift around us all – our mission is to help understand how to find strategic opportunities in this world of rapidly evolving digital technologies. We believe that the tools of social science, even dressed as high-theory, can make practical and concrete contributions to what you are building and the goals of human prosperity and flourishing. For you, we offer some tools that might help.

1 The Supertransition Thesis

1.1 Introduction

We are living through a remarkable period of technological change. Blockchain and cryptocurrencies are revolutionising what it means to own and interact with digital assets. Artificial intelligence (AI) – especially since the launch of ChatGPT in late 2022 – is reshaping professional work. Radical advances in cryptography, such as zero-knowledge proofs, promise to reverse a multi-decade long slide away from privacy. The rise of private firms building reusable rockets, most notably but not solely driven by SpaceX, have brought about a second Space Age unforeseeable even a few years ago. The Internet of Things (IoT) – the smart devices that are reshaping how we interact with the industrial world – give us incredibly precise control over our homes and offices. And we are on the cusp of viable quantum computing that could revolutionise the economy overnight – or, by undermining many of the encryption methods that are used by the technology industry, break it apart.

What is remarkable is not just the magnitude of the changes brought about by these individual and discrete technologies. It is the fact that we are experiencing all these changes *at the same time*. Governments, businesses, communities, and individuals are adopting, and have to adapt to, the simultaneous introduction of blockchain, AI, IoT, the low earth orbit (LEO) economy, advanced cryptography, and quantum computing. As these technologies are brought together they create more disruption to the way the economy – now a *digital economy* – functions at its most fundamental level.

This Element is about the evolution of the digital economy. Our particular way of framing this is through the lens of two deep processes of economic dynamics: *technological change* and *institutional change*. The first is the evolutionary process by which new technologies are created and adopted. The second is the evolutionary process of the creation and adoption of new institutions – that is, rules. We argue that these evolutionary dynamics need to be unified in order to properly understand the digital economy. Our way of unifying them is what we call the *supertransition thesis*, which is the argument that the correct focus of analysis is the cluster of digital technologies – distributed computing in all its forms – and their complex interactions. The supertransition is all of these innovation trajectories *at once, together*.

We are right now on the early part of the curve of a digital economy revolution that is fundamentally multiplicative rather than additive. The algebra that governs the supertransition is not the *sum* of each technology and the innovation trajectory it brings (tech + tech + tech). It is how they interact and feed back on each other – that is, to their *product* (tech x tech x tech). For example, the impact of quantum search and generative AI on economic organisation combined is more substantial than each considered and added individually. This Element concentrates on how frontier technologies interact with each other, because the supertransition is more than the sum of its parts. To understand the supertransition thesis in this way is to understand the revolutionary nature of what is happening in the digital economy today, and to understand how we will supertransition to a more open, global, and complex digital economy over the coming years.

We call it the supertransition because the digital economy thus understood will have a profound effect on the organisation of the economy. In combination, these technologies have *institutional effects*. They change how we organise people and trade, rather just the goods and services we trade. And they do so in a diverse way – we will get more diverse institutions that are competing with each other. Previously slow-changing parameters – namely institutions – are becoming fast-changing variables. This requires a shift from an analytic framework of technology vectors (waves, cycles, innovation processes) to a more 'general equilibrium' perspective in which we consider everything at once to better understand the total effect.

1.2 The Technology Supertransition

When economists talk about technology they are not talking about science or engineering, or any specific uses of technology, even new technologies, but about a more abstract process of change in the economic system: namely, 'technological innovation' and how that will change the established patterns of economic activity. When we talk about technology we are always talking about a process of change, of innovation and disruption. For instance, the 'industrial revolution' was marked by the arrival of a cluster of powerful, disruptive new technologies (in textile machinery, steam engines and railways, etc.), as well as organisational and institutional technologies such as the factory system of production and financial capital. We mark the diffusion of those innovations around the world as the growth of industrialisation.

A *supertransition* is a type of change, and a type of *revolution*, in the sense of a 'turning on an axis', marking a before-and-after period, due to substantial new things in the world. It is a *transition*, namely a passing from one state to another, of something becoming something else, through a process of transition, but which is *super* (Latin: above, over, beyond), and so both a bundle of such processes and that has ramifying consequences. Our theory of the digital supertransition in this Element will describe the dynamics of fundamental change around how economic activity is organised, blurring and undermining boundaries between firms, between resources like capital and labour, and between geopolitical and subnational jurisdictions.

We consider five technologies: artificial intelligence, blockchain, advanced cryptography, quantum computing, and low earth orbit and sensors. Each of these technologies is rapidly advancing in terms of investment, adoption, and technological complexity. This is not an Element explaining the technical details of each of these technology vectors. What matters is how each of those technologies helps to propel the process of institutional acceleration and the supertransition.

Our theory is that the age we are in now is an age of a particular type of supertransition in *institutional technologies*. The economic value that these technologies produce has deep institutional effects in the ways that we organise economic, social, and political production. This is an idea that we have written about before, in the specific context of blockchain technology (Davidson et al. 2018, Berg et al. 2019, Allen et al. 2020), and this Element builds squarely on that insight. But our purpose here is to develop that idea on a much broader plane of a bunch of digital technologies (which we will outline in Section 2) are converging and interacting and driving a powerful transformation of economic institutions, and, moreover, this is happening right now. We outline the economic product of five of these technologies in Table 1.

It will be worthwhile for us to briefly reflect on why this idea is new and different. The standard model of technological change in economic systems is the industrial model. This has been developed by many, but is perhaps best captured in Joseph Schumpeter's vision of technological change as an evolutionary innovative process, driven by entrepreneurial firms, supported by venture finance, following an *innovation trajectory*, which in turn drives *industrial dynamics* in firms and markets, and results in an evolutionary market process of *creative destruction*. This is the standard theory of capitalist dynamics. And it's all true. But that's not the whole story of technological change.

Table 1 The economic product of frontier technologies

Technology	Economic product
Blockchains (including smart contracts, tokens)	Trust
Artificial Intelligence (AI)	Prediction
Quantum Computing	Compute
Advanced Cryptography (e.g. Zero Knowledge Proofs)	Privacy
Low Earth Orbit (LEO) satellites and IoT Sensors	Connectivity

Capitalist dynamics also play out at the level of institutions. Institutions are also technologies. Where industrial technologies mostly organise things, institutional technologies mostly organise people. In the language of micro-theory, institutions are 'coordinating mechanisms'. Sometimes they are both, as with computers and network switching gear and software and screens that are the hard technologies of a stock exchange, but that encodes the rules and laws and routines that coordinate the price discovery and liquidity creation that supports the allocation of capital by millions of investors. A market is both a physical and an institutional technology. And so institutional technologies can also evolve and develop with both new rules and coordination mechanisms, and with new physical instantiations of those, for instance, from open-cry pits of humans shouting at each other using sign language and chalk, to all-electronic platforms that receive digital bids.

Economists have long known that institutional technologies matter enormously to economic performance (see especially the work of Douglass North, who built on Ronald Coase's theory of transaction costs). Yet at the same time they have also mostly ignored dynamics in these things, except where it is of historical or special interest, for the simple reason that institutional technologies tend to change very slowly and can mostly be ignored to focus on much more important economic variables, such as firms, markets, money, capital, prices, or the actions of government and consequences of law. Institutions can be chosen, as if from a menu, but they cannot be created in anything other than the longue durée of history.

Except that sometimes institutional technologies do not change slowly. This is, we think, what is happening now. A set of institutional technologies are changing rapidly as a consequence of a cluster of digital technologies all riding the same explosion of cheap compute and deeply installed hardware. This has not been planned or designed by anyone or any organisation. It is an emergent outcome of the market, a catallaxy of technology supertransition.

We illustrate the relationship between institutions, innovation, technology, and economic growth in Figure 1. It begins with institutions, which create an environment that allows innovation to flourish. Effective institutions create an environment where entrepreneurs and organisations can invest and develop new technologies, as well as experiment with them in the world to create innovative applications. They can plan to make bets on providing value in the future. That the combination of institutions and innovation is the fundamental driver of economic growth and prosperity is one of the least controversial positions of economics, stemming from Adam Smith through the mainline of economics including Friedrich Hayek, Joseph Schumpeter, Douglass North, Joel Mokyr, Deirdre McCloskey, Daron Acemoglu, and James Robinson. The relationship

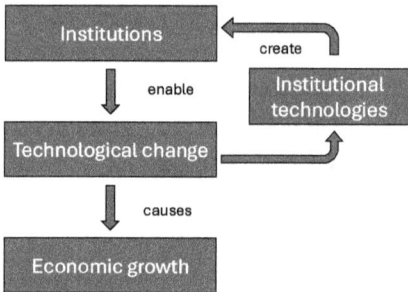

Figure 1 The evolutionary model of institutional technologies

between better institutions and innovation is one that has pulled us out of grinding poverty to unprecedented global wealth and living standards.

Our contribution in this Element is not to argue further for this process, or even to debate it, but to argue that it is rapidly speeding up because of a new feedback loop on the right of the diagram. Technologies are becoming more institutional (allowing for the rapid creation of new institutions), which in turn enables further technological change and growth. The feedback loop suggests a mutually reinforcing relationship where institutions and technological progress evolve together, promoting sustained economic development. The resulting process is an acceleration of institutional creation and technological change.

1.3 Institutional Acceleration

Institutional acceleration is the process whereby digital technologies enable rapid innovation and evolution of economic institutions, leading to faster changes in the rules and mechanisms that coordinate economic activity. This acceleration is driven by the combinatorial nature of digital technologies and their ability to create new forms of economic organisation and governance. Not only are we experiencing a technological upgrade of economic institutions, but that process is accelerating – it is getting faster because of a feedback loop between technologies, institutions, and technological combinatorics. Not only is this technological upgrade of economic institutions happening right now, such that we have technology-driven institutional dynamics, but that it is accelerating. That acceleration has consequences. As a philosophy of technology and as an approach to economics, this is institutional accelerationism, which we will refer to in shorthand as *i/acc* (described in Section 7).

Where physical technologies have many ways to create and accelerate change – consider all of the support mechanisms of innovation – institutional orders are generally exceedingly hard to change. Institutional change is generally figured on historical time scales of cultural and sociopolitical change, not at the speed of frontier technological innovation. And yet, here we are, in a new era where that change is accelerating. The supertransition is the forcing function, and institutional acceleration is the result. So, why is this? What has changed about the world to bring this strange phenomenon to being?

That combinatorial explosion is made possible by digitisation. When a technology transitions from analogue to digital, there are economies of scale and scope. A digital something can be informationally compressed and computed. It can run faster and cheaper. That makes it better on many margins, as we have seen with product after product and industry after industry. But digitisation has a second effect owing to anything digital being able, *mutatis mutandis*, to talk to anything else digital. Digital is a lingua franca – digital things can be encapsulated and made modular and composable. Digital has, for the first time in human history, made institutional acceleration possible.

1.4 Evolutionary Economics and Institutional Acceleration

Biological evolution is based on the genetic replicator – the gene. A gene is a unit of knowledge, a set of molecular instructions for how to make an organic something. Economic evolution is also based on knowledge replicators – rules for making things (technology), rules for actions (economic behaviours, routines, capabilities), and rules for coordination (institutions). Evolutionary economics studies the evolution of technologies, behaviours, and capabilities, with the population-dynamic model of an adoption-diffusion trajectory analytically representing the process of change in 'economic genes' (Nelson and Winter 1982). The modern theory of economic evolution emphasises technological innovation as a process of population dynamics, which can explain changes at different scales, including micro changes in firms, meso changes in markets, industries and clusters, and macro changes in technological regimes and large-scale transitions (Dopfer and Potts 2007). In this framework, clusters of technologies, such as digital technology, are treated as a higher-order trajectory (i.e. a technological regime). Institutions tend to be treated similarly, as macro regimes that describe the selection environment.

While past analyses of technological change often treated institutional evolution as separate or as merely the selection environment, institutional acceleration also represents a coevolutionary dynamic. The concept of coevolution in economics, developed through seminal contributions from Nelson and Winter (1982) and elaborated by scholars like Dopfer and Potts (2007), helps explain this dynamic relationship. As Almudi and Fatas-Villafranca (2021) show, technological and institutional systems evolve together through complex feedback mechanisms that shape their mutual development. Technological recombination and institutional change is a classic coevolutionary dynamic – each not only evolves in response to the other, but the very process of evolution in one domain opens up new evolutionary possibilities in the other. For instance, when entrepreneurs discover new technological combinations, such as integrating blockchain-based voting with AI agents, they also create new institutional possibilities that were previously infeasible. These new institutional forms (e.g. autonomous governance structures) then create fresh opportunities for further technological combinations. This isn't just technological change followed by institutional adaptation, but rather a deeply interconnected process where the evolution of each domain shapes the evolutionary dynamics of the other. This coevolutionary relationship helps us understand institutional acceleration – as technologies and institutions evolve together, they create feedback loops that accelerate the pace of change in both domains.

The concept of a technological supertransition and institutional acceleration that we present here is consistent with the idea of technological trajectories, but with a shift to view this type of economic evolution as a process of innovation that is driving population dynamics of institutional technologies. But the innovation process occurs not only with particular institutional technologies (e.g. blockchain, generative AI) but also in the combinatorial space of these technologies, that is, in the ways they are combined to create new opportunities for economic coordination and value (Arthur 2009).

1.5 Guide to the Element

In Section 2, *Vectors of Technological Change*, we introduce six major technologies that are central to our supertransition to a digital economy. You'll see how artificial intelligence gives us new low-cost prediction machines, blockchains are infrastructure for decentralised trust, advanced cryptography can balance verification and privacy. We'll see how the near future of quantum computing exponentially expands our combinatorial problem-solving capabilities, how the emerging LEO economy enables privately built infrastructure for deep global connectivity, and how advanced manufacturing gives us distributed bespoke production. Our lens through which to view these technologies is how they reshape how we coordinate and organise economic, social, and politics.

Section 3, *Combinatorial Innovation and the Supertransition*, looks at what happens when technologies combine. Combinatorial innovation is counterintuitive and explosive. In this section we examine some early examples of combinatorial innovation. When entrepreneurs combine blockchains with AI, for instance, we see new institutions of decentralised data management, distributed computation, and autonomous economic agents. Integrating IoT with AI creates trusted oracles, making the physical world digital and computable. When LEO satellite imagery uses trusted blockchain infrastructure we end up with new types of distributed capital over ecological ecosystems. These are just the beginning of institutional acceleration – that is the nature of the combinatorial innovation that drives the supertransition. Each of these examples provides new digital institutions within which entrepreneurs can continue to coordinate and innovate in new ways.

In Section 4, *Institutional Acceleration*, we introduce the economic dynamics of combinatorial innovation. While at first these technologies look like industrial technologies, their economic effects are best analysed through the lens of institutional evolution and change. The nature of the technologies we have described breaks down some of the key limits on institutional evolution, namely rigid jurisdiction-based institutions. We explain why these technological combinations are not only propelling institutional change, but also why the pace of change is accelerating. We are building not only new technological combinations, but also new ways to organise ourselves in digital institutions, feeding back into more technological innovation. These institutional impacts of combinatorial innovation expand the space of institutional design and diversity.

In Section 5, *An Economy of Digital Institutions*, we ask what an economy of digital institutions looks like. An economy becomes digital not through new digital technologies alone, but through the development of new and diverse digital institutions. But how are those institutions different from the analogue ones we're familiar with today? The digital economy will be more open. Driven by technologies like blockchains and open-source AI models, this openness will enable freer movement of people and objects across organisational and jurisdictional boundaries. It will also be more complex. That complexity manifests not only in technological complexity, but also in institutional and economic complexity. We're moving into an economy with more choice over more institutions than ever before, and that enables us to drive more computation into our patterns of specialisation and trade. The digital economy will also be more global, where new governing institutions often emerge as global-first platforms and protocols, challenging the traditional ties between institutions and nation-states.

In Section 6, *Adaptation and Agency in the Supertransition*, we ask how you can adapt to the new economic and business environment within which you find yourself. For entrepreneurs, they will need to develop combinatorial alertness, leverage open tools, and pivot from specialists to generalists. Established organisations must grapple with unsupervised shadow combinatorial innovation happening inside their firms, with employees having few incentives to share their productivity-enhancement discoveries. At the same time firms will need to transition to more open and composable organisational structures, enabling their organisation to combine with knowledge and technologies outside of it. Policymakers face an exacerbated pacing problem (the long-time problem of regulators keeping up with technology), requiring a shift towards permissionless innovation and institutional experimentation. For individual workers they must embrace entrepreneurial thinking, diversify income streams, and become more agentic.

Section 7, *Institutional Accelerationism (i/acc)*, makes the case not only for acknowledging institutional acceleration but also for embracing it through institutional accelerationism – or what we call i/acc. Rapid institutional acceleration is fundamentally positive. It gives us more choice in the institutions under which we live. Over the long run, institutional evolution is all that matters. Finding better institutions is what drives more computation and knowledge into our economic system, bringing us more growth and prosperity.

2 Vectors of Technological Change

2.1 Introduction

Technologies are ideas made real. They are knowledge wrested from the universe and formed into valuable materials and useful actions. They evolve as we discover how knowledge can be embedded in them. Because of all this, economies are made of technologies, and technological change causes economic change.

This growth of knowledge process has been going on around the world for many thousands of years now. Economists study 'the rate and direction of technical change', examining institutional incentives for innovation.[1] Historians and anthropologists also view technological change as a historical, social, and cultural phenomenon. And technological change appears to be evolutionary (e.g. see Schumpeter 1939, Rosenberg 1982, Basalla 1988, Mokyr 1990, Ziman 2000, Arthur 2009).

But how do technologies evolve? Technologies 'arrive' through need, inspiration, creativity, luck, dedicated investment, and so on. They are 'differentially adopted and replicated' by the economy (selection), in proportion to their worth, and then put to use (retained, replicated). They exist on a power-law scale – billions have existed, most small and local, but fewer that are revolutionary and global (like fire, metallurgy, and steam engines).

---

[1] As a famous conference and book by Ken Arrow and Richard Nelson from 1962 put it – all modern theories of economic growth are fundamentally accounts of the process of technological change, for example, Solow (1956), Romer (1990), Nelson and Winter (1982).

Since technologies are mostly made of other technologies, they cluster and come in waves. At any one time, clusters of promising frontier technologies move from invention to economic innovation. The industrial revolution brought coal and steam power, steel, and precision instruments. Later came advanced machine tooling, petrochemicals, and internal combustion engines. Still later came transistors and software. Earlier waves included printing presses, double entry bookkeeping, insurance, and writing. And before then codes of law and cities.

This Element is about today's frontier technologies and why they matter. Scholars, scientists, investors, journalists, and politicians have broad agreement about what constitutes this frontier. In line with this, our claim is that a cluster of advanced digital (software-based) technologies – AI, crypto, sensor automation and global networks, quantum compute, digital distributed manufacturing – represent this frontier. Few would disagree that these frontier technologies are powerful, important, valuable, and disruptive. But the deeper, harder question is – how?

Our claim is that they are most powerful, valuable, and disruptive when taken together, and cross-wired into each other. When they *combine*. We'll explore this in Section 3, after we get a sense of what they actually are here. They are all, in different ways, part of a larger emergent system of distributed economic compute. These technologies are digital and software-based. They are all possible because compute is now extremely cheap and available at a massive scale. When combined, these technologies build new types of systems that can coordinate almost arbitrary configurations of people and machines into complex value structures – in other words, they build economies.

2.2 Artificial Intelligence

Artificial intelligence (AI) describes computer systems that perform tasks typically requiring human intelligence: problem-solving, pattern recognition, decision-making, and language understanding. AI's evolution has paralleled computing history, with pioneers like Charles Babbage and Ada Lovelace contemplating AI alongside their computing developments in the mid nineteenth century (Turing 1950, Babbage 2010).

Computing historians often identify distinct AI generations: the first generation (1950s–60s) used formal logic and rule-based systems (e.g. *if-then* rules); the second built expert systems with encoded domain knowledge; and the third (1990s) employed statistical models to 'learn' patterns from data. Each generation represented a shift from rigid predefined rules towards more flexible approaches

Agrawal et al. (2018, 2022) describe AI systems as 'prediction machines'. These systems take an input and make a prediction about what the expected output will be. While early generations relied on manually encoded logic, modern systems use deep learning to predict likely outputs based on training data.

Prediction systems have been implemented in business and government for decades, such as identifying fraudulent transactions. But ChatGPT's release in November 2022 was a dramatic event in the history of AI. Both technical and non-technical audiences saw unprecedented capabilities in knowledge and creative output through large language models trained via machine learning and human feedback. Along with AI projects that can create high-quality images and high-quality human-like speech from text and image inputs, this class of 'generative AI' has captured the attention of consumers, firms, and policymakers. We focus on it in this section in part because of that public salience, but also because it clearly demonstrates the institutional effects of AI as a transformative economic technology.

These are two critical economic dimensions of generative AI revolution that have implications for institutional acceleration: (1) the impact on productivity and (2) the dynamic between open and closed source generative AI models.

Generative AI has brought about significant productivity benefits across the economy. Brynjolfsson et al. (2023) found that customer service agents using AI assistance handled inquiries more effectively. Tools like GitHub Copilot have enhanced programmer productivity, with one study showing a 26 per cent improvement using a relatively early generative AI model (Cui et al. 2024). AI-assisted writing tools have enabled professionals in journalism, academia, marketing, and content creation to draft and edit text more efficiently – including, of course, writing this Element. These productivity gains have complex distributional effects. Generative AI may raise the productivity of the least productive workers, while only adding marginal benefits to top performers (Brynjolfsson et al. 2023).

Perhaps more significant for institutional acceleration are the dynamics of open and closed source AI models. Frontier models require significant capital investment to build and operate, favouring proprietary and closed systems such as OpenAI's GPT, which charged for centralised infrastructure access. But the fully open-source 2022 release of StabilityAI's Stable Diffusion image generation model radically shifted the economics of generative AI. Hobbyists and start-ups leveraged this platform to develop diverse AI applications. Similarly, Meta's LLaMA model (2023) spawned numerous open-source chat models, challenging closed systems like ChatGPT.

Open-source models have profound impacts on innovation, competition, and regulation. A leaked 2023 memo by a Google employee (whose authenticity has not been confirmed but not rejected) argued that open-source was likely to outcompete closed-source generative AI through distributed tinkering and rapid use-case improvements ('Google: "We Have No Moat,"' 2023). Business demands also favour customisable open-source models that can be adapted – open-source models can be brought 'in house', customised to proprietary data, and controlled with bespoke governance. Open-source AI not only shifts economic and technical power away from the firms that outlay the investment in model development, but it also complicates regulatory efforts. Open-source AI introduces an institutional limit to how effective such control can be.

2.3 Blockchain

Distributed data sharing wasn't novel when Satoshi Nakamoto (2008) introduced blockchain technology through bitcoin. Google, for example, used a number of globally distributed systems that replicate data across multiple servers (e.g. see Corbett et al. 2013). These consensus mechanisms, such as Paxos, come to agreement over the replicated data. What Nakamoto developed was the decentralisation of consensus through a blockchain. Blockchains are distributed computers that come to consensus over replicated data without the authority of a third-party. In Bitcoin, anyone can participate permissionlessly (Nabben and Zargham 2022) in the consensus process by becoming a 'miner', receiving bitcoin tokens as an incentive to participate.

The blockchain industry has expanded with numerous chains competing on privacy, speed, and security, using various consensus mechanisms beyond Bitcoin's 'proof of work'. A key feature of blockchains is their 'censorship resistance' through decentralised consensus – no single authority can prevent network validation without overwhelming control of the network. In Bitcoin, this would require controlling 51 per cent of the network's economic weight.

Censorship resistance is economically meaningful. In *Understanding the Blockchain Economy*, we explain how blockchain economises on trust in exchange (Berg et al. 2019, see also Davidson et al. 2018). Following the Nobel laureate Oliver Williamson, we view economic institutions as mechanisms to reduce transaction costs. Blockchain's social consensus mitigates opportunistic behaviour from counterparties to exchange. A simple transaction that is conducted through blockchain infrastructure limits the ability for any party to renege on their side of the agreement, making agreements self-enforcing rather than relying on legal systems.

Because blockchains are programmable, they have a wide variety of applications. While originally developed to create the digital cash Bitcoin, any computationally describable economic coordination can utilise blockchain's censorship-resistant properties through 'smart contracts' (Allen and Lane 2024). Blockchain applications have spread across art, property registries, supply chain management, prediction markets, gaming, credentials, scientific research, environmental renewal, and organisational governance.

Blockchain's institutional impact is most evident in decentralised finance, or 'defi' (see Mohan 2022). Defi protocols create financial products using decentralised mechanisms. For instance, decentralised exchanges enable cryptocurrency trading through user-provided asset pools. The defi ecosystem is expanding but includes systems of lending, borrowing, margin, and derivative products, offering tokenised assets that users can combine across protocols for complex financial strategies.

The decentralised nature of these applications means defi operates under fundamentally different institutional assumptions than traditional finance. First, defi is *global-first*. Unlike traditional banks which launch and expand jurisdiction-by-jurisdiction, defi applications are instantly accessible worldwide on global blockchain networks. Second, defi is *pseudonoymous*. Blockchain applications lack native identity verification systems that link on-chain activities to real-world identities. There is little to prevent users from creating multiple blockchain accounts or addresses, creating the 'Sybil problem'. It is difficult to build decentralised products that rely on fixed identities (Douceur 2002) such as under collateralised lending (Harwick and Caton 2022). Third, defi is *non-hierarchical*. Decentralised finance is decentralised. Applications typically adopt democratic or quasi-democratic structures, contrasting with traditional financial hierarchies. This context has spurred innovations like decentralised autonomous organisations (see Allen et al. 2023). Finally, defi is *non-custodial*. Users maintain direct asset control, subject to protocol rules and smart contracts, unlike centralised finance where assets are typically held by service providers or dedicated custody firms.

These different assumptions create unique opportunities for innovation, enabling novel products like self-repaying loans and automated market makers with self-rebalancing asset pools. But these innovations also challenge existing regulatory frameworks which have been built around assumptions of centralisation. Policies often address risks specific to centralised finance (e.g. custodial misuse) that simply don't exist in defi. In this way blockchain technology both enables institutional experimentation and necessitates rethinking financial governance and regulation.

2.4 Cryptography

Cryptography has historically developed mostly for the use of military and diplomatic authorities, serving as a vital tool for securing sensitive communications and maintaining strategic advantages. Ancient military authorities used simple substitution ciphers to conceal messages, while more sophisticated polyalphabetic ciphers, like the fifteenth-century Vigenère cipher, used multiple substitution alphabets based on a key, improving resistance to frequency analysis.

Commercial cryptography expanded significantly with nineteenth-century telecommunications, as businesses needed to protect information transmitted over telegraph lines. Throughout the twentieth century, commercial cryptography often led military applications – the German Enigma machine, famously targeted by UK's Bletchley Park, was originally developed for commercial transactions (Kahn 1967).

Post-WWII there were new demands on cryptographical security and the use of cryptography for exchange. Modern cryptography was co-developed at the same time as Claude Shannon's information theory that provides the backbone of digital communication.[2] The modern cryptographic landscape was shaped by three key milestones: (1) the creation of the Data Encryption Standard (DES), which demonstrated how national security interests could constrain commercial cryptography development; (2) the breakthrough development of asymmetric cryptography by Diffie and Hellman (1976), which enabled secure communication without pre-shared keys and laid the foundation for digital commerce; and (3) the resolution of the 'Crypto Wars' in the 1990s, where cypherpunks and business interests successfully challenged NSA attempts to control cryptographic development, leading to the establishment of open cryptographic standards that now underpin much of our digital economy.

The field of cryptographic research is ultimately a field of creating new systems of property rights over information – and through it over digital assets. Rogaway (2015) argues that cryptography 'rearranges power: it configures who can do what, from what'. While this captures the political dimensions of cryptography, our claim is that the reconfiguration of power is, prior to its political and ethical dimensions, a fundamentally economic reconfiguration. New developments in cryptography change the environment by which exchanges can occur. This ability of cryptography to create new institutions and property rights is evident in the milestones considered earlier. Asymmetric cryptography allowed economically valuable exchanges to occur between mutually mistrusting parties, facilitating the growth of digital commerce,

---

[2] See the comments in Hellman and Yost (2014).

which in turn was ultimately the argument which won the political debate over access to cryptography in the 1990s.

Zero knowledge proofs (ZKPs) are a cryptographic standard that allows individuals to demonstrate knowledge of knowledge without revealing any of the knowledge itself. We can prove that we know something without having to reveal the information that it is we know. First proposed in 1985, they offer a vision of the world where we can fully exploit the information we have about ourselves without leaking information to others (that they might choose to exploit without our consent).

In an economic environment where data is both extremely valuable and highly sensitive, the suggestion that we might be able to demonstrate the existence of data without revealing that data has revolutionary institutional implications. Consider being able to use ZKPs to demonstrate creditworthiness to a bank. Rather than exposing all your transaction data to a credit assessment officer, and hence potentially revealing to them all the sometimes intimate information that can be inferred from credit card purchases (as well as those that can be gained from knowing your salary, employer, work history, and so forth), a ZKP creditworthiness system could calculate the banks creditworthiness assessment on a user's device and then communicate solely the result of that calculation to the bank. These applications address growing privacy concerns in an increasingly data-hungry private sector, where every information request risks privacy breachers and potential identity theft.

2.5 Quantum Computing

The intellectual origins of quantum computing trace back to the development of quantum mechanics in the early twentieth century, which describes the behaviour of matter and energy at atomic and subatomic levels. While classical computing relies on bits – binary units that are either 0 or 1 – to process information, quantum computing uses qubits, which can exist in multiple states simultaneously through superposition and entanglement. Yuri Manin first seriously considered quantum computing in 1980. In *Computable and Uncomputable*, Manin suggested that quantum mechanics could be harnessed for computation, noting classical computers' limitations in simulating quantum systems. Richard Feynman (1982, 1986) expanded on this idea in the 1980s, proposing that quantum computers would be better suited for simulating quantum phenomena and overcoming the computational limits of classical machines, especially for tasks involving large-scale quantum systems. David Deutsch (1985) later formalised the concept of a 'universal quantum computer', demonstrating their potential to solve certain problems exponentially faster than classical computers.

Currently, quantum computing remains in early development. With at least eight major systems being developed globally, no quantum computer has been developed at sufficient scale to meaningfully displace classical computation for any given task (Bremner et al. 2024). Nevertheless, ongoing algorithm development allows us to forecast quantum computation's impact given current knowledge.

Shor (1994) provided the first demonstration of a quantum algorithm solving a problem exponentially faster than any known classical algorithm. Shor's algorithm employs quantum mechanics to factor large integers efficiently. But this quantum advantage applies only to specific mathematical tasks. Grover's algorithm (1996) demonstrated a more general and prospective quantum advantage, using quantum superposition to search an unsorted database quadratically faster than classical algorithms.

The implications of Grover's algorithms are potentially more significant.[3] In a world of cheaper search, more search will be consumed. While a classical computer requires 1,000,000 steps to search an unstructured list of 1,000,000 entries, a mature quantum computer using Grover's algorithm would need only about 1,000 steps. Bova, Goldfarb, and Melko (2021) describe this search capability generally as a potential advantage at solving combinatorics problems, where the goal is to search through all possible arrangements of a set of items to find specific criteria-meeting configurations. Although error correction and quantum architecture costs might reduce quantum computers' search advantage, these represent engineering hurdles rather than permanent constraints.

Search is a transaction cost that raises the cost of mutually beneficial exchange (Stigler 1961, Roth 1982). Both buyers and sellers face search costs. Much economic organisation is unsurprisingly structured around reducing search costs, demonstrated by the digital platform economy. Multi-sided markets like eBay match buyers with sellers at global scale, facilitating trades that high search costs would otherwise prevent.

Quantum computing offers a massive reduction in transaction costs. Such a substantial decrease in search costs would likely have a correspondingly large transformation on the structure of economic activity. Search costs partially explain why firms and individuals prefer to own resources rather than access them through markets – owned assets are more readily utilisable than seeking market rentals. Put another way, lowering search costs favours outsourcing rather than ownership ('buy' in the market, rather than 'make' in-house). They also have

---

[3] This section is partly derived from Berg and Potts (2024).

a globalising effect, enabling economic actors to explore broader possibilities for exchange. This has the effect of increasing the size of the market, which (as Adam Smith tells us) increases specialisation and the gains from trade. In this way, quantum computing powers economic growth.

Compute is a commodity. Just as buyers of coal or electricity are ultimately buying embodied energy, compute buyers are ultimately buying a reduction in the time it takes to perform a computational task (Davies 2004). Some tasks favour classical computers, others quantum computers, and some can be satisfied by either. Users should be indifferent to the origin of their compute, focusing instead on meeting their computational needs within budget and time constraints. This indifference between classical and quantum sources significantly influences how quantum computing capability is distributed amongst firms and geopolitical powers.

From major cloud services to personal devices, for computational tasks where classical computers dominate, compute is already massively decentralised. There is no barrier to competition in classical compute, nor any risk of one geopolitical actor dominating. Where bottlenecks in classical compute emerge are in the production networks for semiconductor chips – a known problem with a known menu of policy stances and responses. Similarly, no such risk emerges around computational tasks where classical or quantum systems are equally suited.

A major institutional impact of quantum computing development is its challenge to dominant cryptographic standards. Shor's algorithm's ability to factor large integers threatens systems like RSA that rely on prime factorisation for security. Post-quantum encryption algorithms, designed to resist both classical and quantum attacks, use alternative mathematical problems such as lattice-based or multivariate polynomial problems. However, updating real-world cryptographic systems poses significant challenges given quantum computing's uncertain timeline. The cryptography threat offers insight into frontier technology interactions. Since harmful encryption breaches often occur covertly, their impact may remain hidden. However, blockchain markets' use of vulnerable cryptography could serve as an early warning system – the Bitcoin price potentially acting as a leading indicator of quantum supremacy (Rohde et al. 2021).

2.6 Satellites, Low Earth Orbit, IoT, Sensors

All economies invest heavily in transport and communications infrastructure. Empire economies were built on roads, ports, and ships. The industrial revolution accelerated connectivity through rail networks in the nineteenth century, followed by highways and air transport in the twentieth. The 1800s saw electrical signals science evolve into global telecommunications networks of relays, radio towers, and undersea cables to move data.

The space age emerged with rocketry development, advanced control systems, and digital communication, marked by TelStar's 1962 launch as the first commercial communication satellite. Yet space access remained government-controlled due to national security priorities and industry funding structures. Commercial space use was heavily regulated, with market involvement tightly linked to defence contracting (Weinzierl 2018).

Today, the private sector, particularly innovative start-ups, dominates space access. MacDonald (2017) argues that this is actually a return to a longer run pattern of private funding of exploration. Weinzierl (2023) argues that the modern turn to the private sector is due to institutional policy reform in the early 2000s, including the reforms towards fixed-price contracting (away from the weak innovation incentives of traditional cost-plus contracting and direct agency oversight). These changes 'led to a surge in private-sector entrepreneurship, investment and success'.

SpaceX, a private company founded in 2002, have launched almost two-thirds of the 10,000 or so satellites currently in orbit through Starlink. Through innovative engineering, civilian-grade electronics, and entrepreneurial energy, a new generation of space companies has massively lowered the cost of access to space. The emergence of the low earth orbit economy has been a private global economic infrastructure revolution (Vance 2023, Weinzierl 2023).

Two examples illustrate this transformation to private space infrastructure. Planet Labs, founded in 2010 by former NASA researchers, revolutionised satellite imaging by using villain-grade electronics in their cubesats to make cheap satellites capable of daily global imaging. Meanwhile, in New Zealand, amateur rocket builder Peter Beck launched RocketLabs in 2006, achieving orbit with its low-cost Electron rocket in 2018, growing into a multinational space vehicle enterprise. Many other companies like these are building the LEO space economy above our heads.

The LEO space economy is booming, with projected growth to US$300 billion by 2035 (Deloitte Space 2022, Highfill and Weinzierl 2024). Core components include advanced technology infrastructure and services – vehicle manufacture, rocket launches, cargo, and operations – provided by companies like SpaceX and Rocket Labs.

Demand for LEO services spans multiple sectors. The base market of LEO is satellite communications (mostly for backhaul). The remote sensing market is expanding rapidly. These are both particularly valuable for much of the world's agriculture and mining, especially for robotic automation requiring low latency.

The Starlink constellation extends internet coverage to everywhere on earth, including oceans, mountains, and sky (i.e. on ships, in aircraft), which transforms the economic possibilities of remote regions and non-territorial domains.

Launch costs continue to fall because of recyclable vehicles and scale economies. Safety is improving through materials and operations innovation. These improvements are transforming the prospects for new industries in space tourism (sub-orbital and orbital), and also in space research and manufacturing to exploit, for example, the properties of materials and processes in microgravity. Further along the frontier are large-scale manufacturing and infrastructure (e.g. orbital compute clusters for AI), as well as asteroid-mining for materials for lunar or Martian colonisation.

LEO is a frontier economy. The rise of commercial space is due to a major institutional shift from public missions to private entrepreneurship. The business opportunities in the LEO economy are mostly on earth, and, as we will see in the following sections, these satellites are a foundational infrastructure that combines with the other frontier technologies we have discussed earlier.

3 Combinatorial Innovation and the Supertransition

3.1 Introduction

The standard approach to understanding the frontier technologies described earlier would be to take each and apply theories and measurements grounded in innovation trajectories. That approach would consider a technology and look at its adoption rates, market penetration, and potential economic impacts in isolation. The tools would be S-curve models or diffusion theories to predict future growth and societal integration. In this Element we chart a different approach: applying the lens of combinatorial innovation. When blockchain technology interacts with artificial intelligence, or when quantum computing enhances cryptographic systems, we enter an economic context where technologies, each powerful in its own right, are mixed and recombined to create novel arrangements that are *more than the sum of their parts*. Our aim in this section is both to explain combinatorial innovation and to show that it is happening.

3.2 Combinatorial Innovation

3.2.1 What Is Combinatorics?

The dominant model of technological innovation in the modern era is the trajectory, or wave. This approach views innovation as the vector of the adoption of an idea into a population. Roger (1962) exemplifies the classic study of innovation trajectories. These trajectories form the analytic foundation of historical narratives of technology driving economic dynamics (Schumpeter 1939, Soete and Freeman 2012).

Humans find trajectories easy to think about. They are measurable and visualisable. They conform to a classic story arc: *origination* (the disruptive hero), *adoption* (goes on a journey, changing the world), *retention* (order is restored). We can easily formulate a trajectory of, say, computers or smartphones into the economy. Trajectories are familiar, intuitive, and predictable. But institutional acceleration is not to be understood as one, several, or even many individual trajectories. Rather, it is a fundamentally *combinatorial process*. Our human minds, shaped by linear experiences and parochial perspectives, often struggle to comprehend the explosive potential of combinatorial processes.

We humans are not wired to think combinatorially. Even extremely smart and intellectually courageous people such as your authors still struggle to visualise even simple combinatorial phenomena such as compound interest (i.e. self-combinatorics) and just how fast things can grow. Consider we place $1 on the first square of a chessboard, and double it until the 64th square – how much money is on the board? Most people will correctly guess 'a lot', but few will grasp the actual magnitude, as orders of magnitude more money than has ever existed in all of human history and perhaps across the universe combined. The answer is $18,446,744,073,709,551,615. Combinatorial processes quickly lead to counterintuitive outcomes.

Combinatorics can produce results that seem to defy conventional logic due to the massive state spaces they create – an enormous set of possible outcomes or states that grow exponentially with each added element. Compounding this is the concept of *re-combinatorics*, where new things (made from combinations) feed back into the pool to further recombine. This process can start small, yet rapidly produce extremely large and complex outcomes. A good understanding of combinatorial spaces is essential for evolutionary thinking, as highly improbable phenomena can hide in sufficiently vast state spaces. It is also important for entrepreneurial strategy, as economic opportunities hide in those spaces too.

Part of the challenge in the context of combinatorics is how to discover value in such a large space. Both natural and economic systems rely on mechanisms to sift through vast combinatorial spaces. In biology, we have natural selection. In economic systems we rely on processes such as market competition as a selection mechanism. Entrepreneurs experiment with various combinations of technologies, business models, and institutional arrangements, then those that create value survive and proliferate, while less successful combinations fade away.

3.2.2 Institutional Combinatorics

For centuries we have happily lived in a space of combinatorial innovation with *industrial technologies*. Economists of technology and economic growth have repeatedly explained this.[4] The combination of the steam engine with wheeled transport, for instance, gave us railways. Joseph Schumpeter famously described this process of industrial combinatorics as one of 'creative destruction', showing how new combinations of technologies and business models continuously reshape the economic system.

But we have little experience with or even intuition about combinatorics unfolding over *institutional technologies*. Recent work by evolutionary anthropologists highlights the historical variety in ancestral institutions, contrasting with the alleged institutional monoculture of modern economies (Graeber and Wengrow 2021). We modern humans are not used to economic institutions changing rapidly. Not politically, not culturally, not cognitively.

We are today entering an era of combinatorial innovation in institutional technologies. This shift is opening up an inestimably large space for new economic institutions. Combinatorial innovation in institutional technologies (digital, composable, global technologies) is the mechanism that drives institutional acceleration. In Table 2 we outline some of these combinations. The vast scale of this new institutional universe might generate some mild terror.

The first implication is the need for *institutional modularity and composability* – a principle fundamental to industrialisation, mass production, and innovation (Walsh 2006). And, as Herbert Simon (1962) explains, modularity is key to the architecture of complexity. Yet this concept of modular institutions initially seems odd, as we traditionally view institutions as monolithic legacies of culture, law, or geography. They are typically supplied by monopolistic governments, rather than as modular, composable economic goods. Blockchains are clear examples of institutions as modular and composable economic goods. Decentralised finance (DeFi) offers components such as token standards, automated market makers, stablecoins, decentralised exchanges, and oracles. These are often called 'money legos'. The institution of money is able to be unbundled into a set of modular technologies that can be combined and recomposed in surprising and innovative ways. Then each component becomes a site for competition and innovation.

The second implication is the *development of meta-level systems* for the combinatorics of institutional innovations. While industrial technologies have long benefitted from structured innovation systems, recognising their crucial

---

[4] Theories of technological recombination are an important strand of long-run economic growth theory (e.g. von Neumann 1945, Romer 1986, Weitzman 1998, Arthur 2009, Koppl et al. 2023).

Table 2 Combinatorics overview

Technology	Artificial Intelligence	Quantum Computing	Advanced Cryptography	LEO Satellites & IoT Sensors
Blockchains	• Decentralised markets for training data (Ocean Protocol) • Decentralised markets for compute (Akash Network) • Smart contract constrained generative AI (Berg et al. 2023) • Hyperbarter (Berg et al. 2019) • AI-governed DAOs (Marengo 2024; Nabben 2023, Xu et al. 2023)	• Quantum cryptography-resistant blockchains (Bennett and Brassard 2014) • Quantum money for blockchain scaling (Coladangelo and Sattath 2020) • Distributed quantum internet (Rohde 2021)	• Zero-knowledge privacy money (Zcash) • Zero-knowledge privacy-preserving smart contracts (Penumbra) • Layer 2 blockchains power secured by zero-knowledge proof (Loopring, StarkNet)	• Space information networks (Bao et al. 2021) • Oracle satellites (Regen Network) • Weather oracles (Chainlink) • Supply chain oracles (Moudoud et al. 2019) • Low earth orbit data centres (proposed by Amazon, Nippon Telegraph and Telephone) • Blockchain for data privacy in IoT systems (Marengo 2024)
Artificial Intelligence		• Quantum machine learning (Gujju et al. 2024)	• AI cryptanalysis (Singh et al. 2024) • On-device AI (open-source AI models,	• AI-enhanced Earth observation (Φ-sat−1) • IoT to collect data for AI training

Table 2 (cont.)

Technology	Artificial Intelligence	Quantum Computing	Advanced Cryptography	LEO Satellites & IoT Sensors
			• Apple's Private Cloud Compute • Homomorphic encryption for AI training (Baruch et al. 2022, Arnold et al., 2022) • Secure federated learning (Zhang et al. 2022)	• Smart cities (Lv et al. 2021) • Smart farming (Pal and Joshi 2023)
Quantum Computing			• Quantum cryptanalysis (Grover 1996) • Quantum key distribution (Bennett and Brassard 2014) • Quantum money (Weisner 1983) • Blind quantum computing (Fitzsimons 2017)	• Quantum computing for IoT network optimisation (Bhatia and Sood 2020) • Satellite-based quantum information networks (de Forges de Parney et al. 2023)
Advanced Cryptography				• Secure data trusts through satellites (Wang et al. 2024)

role in driving progress, we lack comparable frameworks for institutional innovation. The most effective model for developing such innovation is likely *evolution* – a process of cheap, parallel, blind search with environmental feedback. In economic contexts, entrepreneurs provide variation through new products and business configurations, while market mechanisms select. This Schumpeterian model sees these evolutionary processes as producing positive spillovers, underling the justification for public support through innovation policy.

Cultural evolution of institutions through rule selection (Hayek 1973, North 1990, 2005, Hodgson 2002, Aoki 2007) can be slow and prone to local optima. Nevertheless this is the predominant form of all cultural evolution (Richerson and Boyd 2005). Industrial evolution has been able to speed this process up and massively improve its efficiency through these Schumpeterian mechanisms of capitalism, namely competitive R&D, venture finance, and entrepreneurship, combined with supportive innovation systems, such as intellectual property rights, publicly funded research, R&D subsidies, and other forms of support (Bloom et al. 2019). Innovation can also emerge through distributed user innovation and local problem-solving (von Hippel 2016), as demonstrated by blockchain and decentralised finance institutional experiments (Buterin et al. 2019, Allen et al. 2023, de Filippi et al. 2024).

To propel institutional combinatorics we need a deeper understanding of both public research initiatives and open innovation approaches, including institutional technology toolkits (Allen and Potts 2023) and innovation commons (Allen and Potts 2016, Potts 2019, Potts et al. 2024). Currently, institutional science remains fragmented across anthropology, economics, law, and politics, focusing more on theory than practical experimentation. While we lack a comprehensive 'library' of institutions and the field remains relatively primitive, the foundational elements are here today. In the following sections we look at what this process of institutional combinatorics looks like in practice: what happens when we rapidly experiment with new institutional technology combinations?

3.3 Blockchains x AI

Blockchain provides a foundational economic layer for the organisation of exchange (Davidson et al. 2018, Berg et al. 2019). What happens when we combine the predictive power of AI with the trust of blockchains? Among other institutional advances, we get training and compute markets, hyperbarter and autonomous agents.

3.3.1 Blockchain for Training Markets

AI requires vast amounts of data to train models that can make accurate predictions. Diverse, high-quality datasets are essential for training robust models. While there are many complexities that have to be navigated, using our current approach to generative AI, the more data is available to train on, the better the models are. As OpenAI's Sam Altman has written, 'To a shocking degree of precision, the more compute and data available, the better it gets at helping people solve hard problems.'[5] The challenge in collecting and controlling data for AI training lies in balancing privacy and security while ensuring access to high-quality datasets. Centralised control risks monopolies, while decentralised sharing faces issues of consent, ownership, and compliance.

One blockchain-enabled AI training program is Ocean Protocol, which uses a blockchain to create a transparent, decentralised system for data sharing and monetisation. Ocean's key innovation is its 'compute-to-data' mechanism, which allows AI algorithms to run on private data without the data leaving its owner, ensuring privacy while enabling AI training on sensitive datasets. Data owners maintain full control and set access terms, with blockchain recording every transaction for accountability. Ocean tokenises data as a digital asset, creating incentives where providers are rewarded for making datasets available, while AI developers can pay for access using Ocean tokens. This model democratises access to high-quality datasets and compute resources, overcoming data monopolies and fostering a more open, secure, and privacy-preserving environment for AI development.

3.3.2 Blockchain for Compute Markets

Another major constraint on AI is access to computational resources, whether for training or using models. At a global level, compute power is not scarce, but it is widely distributed, and the early years of generative AI revealed significant bottlenecks. The high-end GPUs developed for specialised AI use were subject to supply constraints – particularly given NVIDIA's platform dominance in the GPU market – making them expensive and scarce.

What value do blockchains add to shared compute markets? While cloud providers offer compute-as-a-service, blockchains remove reliance on a single provider. This enables a permissionless and competitive marketplace, where anyone can lease unused resources securely and transparently. Blockchains x AI democratise access to computing power through a more open and decentralised alternative to centralised cloud services.

---

[5] https://ia.samaltman.com/.

Decentralised markets using blockchains for compute sharing offer a solution to the bottlenecks of direct ownership or traditional cloud rental. One example is Akash, a decentralised cloud computing platform where users buy and sell unused computing resources through a reverse-auction marketplace. This competition typically yields lower costs, while the platform's Supercloud offers access to high-performance GPUs for AI and machine learning workloads.

3.3.3 Smart Contracts to Constrain Chaotic Robots

Blockchain technology also provides an institutional mechanism to address some of the limitations of current generative AI models. The outputs of large language models are unpredictable, or, as we have described them 'pseudo-nondeterministic'; exhibiting behaviours that can give users the impression of creativity. While this pseudo-nondeterminism is valuable for tasks like writing or coding and explains the human-like interactions possible with generative AI, making them unsuitable for actions that require high levels of surety and security, such as sending emails or interacting with financial systems. We have described this as the 'chaotic robot' problem, where LLMs' pseudo-nondeterministic nature, including tendencies to hallucinate or act contrary to user intentions, creates risks in economically valuable interactions.

Blockchain-based smart contracts provide a solution to the chaotic robot problem. Smart contracts, with their deterministic and immutable properties, could serve as a gating mechanism between LLMs and real-world systems. This would allow LLMs to act within strictly defined parameters, ensuring security and alignment with users' preferences. AI provides creative output while blockchain ensures safe and predictable execution. This contributes to 'economic alignment', solving the principal–agent problem by ensuring that AI acts in accordance with specific user instructions through smart contracts.

3.3.4 Hyperbarter

Blockchains can constrain AI, but also empower it. The technology provides a digital native economic layer for AI to utilise as part of value transfer. Cryptocurrency and other digital assets will be the money that AI uses. The reason for this is not simply that native internet intelligence requires a native internet asset economic layer. Rather, the complex organisational, institutional, and regulatory frameworks that have built up around traditional financial systems and payment networks will be difficult (at least in the medium term) for AI systems to navigate and interface with. It is hard to imagine, for example traditional retail financial organisations, such as Citibank, allowing AI the sort of unfettered access to consumer bank accounts that a fully empowered AI agent might seek. By contrast, blockchain offers such complexity and permissionlessness out-of-the-box.

This observation suggests something significant but the interaction between AI and blockchain. At the limit both AI and blockchain systems are unbounded; that is, they can perform for their users any computable task (subject to resource constraints). This is what is meant by Turing completeness. AI systems are a form of computational system that can perform any task a computational system can perform. And blockchains are little more than distributed and decentralised networks of fully capable computational systems. The boundlessness of these two systems contrasts with the highly bounded and non-digitally native traditional financial and legal system, which is characterised by the constraints imposed on it over centuries. There have been good reasons for those constraints. Practice of constraining the range of possible human activity makes the world legible and provides the institutions for social and economic exchange, but those constraints have been designed for humans – with human motivations and human cognitive limitations. The unbounded capabilities of Turing complete systems make many of these 'artificial' boundaries around what can and cannot be done inappropriate and unnecessarily limiting for autonomous digital exchange.

Consider how cognitive limitations in humans shaped money's evolution as an institution – a tool to solve the inefficiencies of barter systems that were cognitively overwhelming for human minds. However, these limitations don't apply to AI. As Turing complete systems, both blockchain and AI can handle vast permutations of transactions that humans cannot, enabling 'hyperbarter' – a machine-mediated form of exchange that bypasses traditional money (Berg et al. 2018). The inherent flexibility of digital assets on blockchains provides AI with a more fitting economic infrastructure. While money was necessary to reduce cognitive load on human decision-making, AI can navigate a complex space where any tokenised asset can serve as a unit of value, tailored to each transaction. This suggests a future where traditional money may become obsolete for machine-mediated exchanges, as Turing complete systems interact autonomously without the simplifications required by human cognitive constraints.

3.3.5 Autonomous Agents

An autonomous agent is an economic agent. That is, something that can make and execute decisions (it can search for opportunities, buy and sell things, enter into contracts) and does so on behalf of its human principal. It is an agent in the same way that service professionals (accountants, lawyers, real estate brokers) are able to act as agents on your behalf. There is an implicit trust relation that must exist for this to work. Part of that is institutional (licensing arrangements, commercial law agreements, regulatory agencies, courts), but it also requires well-designed mechanisms (reputation, expectations of repeated dealings). The more complex an economy, the more agency it will contain, for such agency relations exist due to the benefits of specialisation and gains from trade.

The limits of agency, however, are not just the cost of the service as specialised compute and scale (e.g. in which a search engine is an agent substitute for a librarian + library). The development of new technologies of agency also requires innovation in alignment with the principal. The combination of smart contracts, to constrain and render agency safe, as well as machine learning to drive deep alignment (e.g. local training on personal and private data of past behaviour) are both institutional solutions that advance the capabilities of artificial agency.

Autonomous economic agents are a radical new object in the economy that lies on the other side of the supertransition. The first uses of them will be as a low-cost substitution for currently high-cost existing economic agency relations: for example, financial advice and management, such as portfolio optimisation or insurance. For that, observe that your finance bot will require permissioned access to your assets and the ability to interact with them. This means they will need to be fully digital real world assets (this is what tokenisation delivers). But when things become cheaper, we use them more, and so agent-based bot trading will explode, disrupting existing economic patterns and creating new economic niches. This is a familiar pattern of the effects of automation on economic and social structure over long periods of time – consider how cheap automobiles in the 1920s eventually caused suburbs and teen culture by the 1950s. The challenge of navigating the supertransition is to think past the initial substitution phenomena to the deeper structural dynamics.

3.4 Combining Other Technologies

3.4.1 Blockchain x IoT

Oracles

An oracle is a trusted third-party service that supplies external data to a blockchain or smart contract, enabling decentralised applications to interact with off-chain resources. Oracles act as intermediaries that provide verifiable and accurate data inputs, which smart contracts use to execute predefined actions. Blockchains are closed off from other networks, allowing them to remain secure from outside interference. This determinism is a feature, not a bug. But smart contracts will often need to utilise data that doesn't exist on the blockchain it is executed on. For instance, a smart contract might require outside data such as the price of another token (e.g. for a swap on a decentralised exchange), the weather in a particular location (e.g. for an insurance claim), or an external decision (e.g. from a dispute resolution process).

Oracles provide a secure way to integrate off-chain data with on-chain smart contracts. Data from IoT devices, APIs, or external databases enables smart contracts to interact with real-world events while maintaining blockchain security. Chainlink, a leading oracle provider, aggregates price data from multiple exchanges through independent nodes, creating reliable on-chain price feeds. These feeds power decentralised finance applications through accurate, tamper-resistant data secured by reputation systems and node staking.

Combining IoT with blockchain to create oracles enables automated systems responding to real-world events. In cold chain logistics, temperature sensors in pharmaceutical shipments transmit data through oracles to blockchain platforms. Smart contracts verify temperature conditions and can automatically trigger alerts if deviations occur. This creates tamper-proof tracking that streamlines operations and builds stakeholder trust.

In contrast to generalised oracle providers like Chainlink, Regen Network focuses specifically on ecological data. Their network relies on 'ecological state verifiers' – ecologists and land stewards who conduct on-ground assessments using soil sampling, biodiversity surveys, and remote sensing. This data on soil carbon, forest health, and water quality feeds into the Regen Ledger blockchain, where smart contracts facilitate ecological agreements. For example, landowners pursuing carbon sequestration can have their efforts verified and quantified, leading to carbon credit issuance on the Regen Network.

Decentralised Physical Infrastructure Networks (DePINs)

Decentralised Physical Infrastructure Networks (DePINs) leverage blockchain technology, tokenised incentives, and the Internet of Things (IoT) to create community-owned networks that challenge traditional centralised infrastructure models. While conventional telecommunications, energy grids, and transportation systems often suffer from high costs, limited access, and centralised control, DePINs distribute ownership and control among network participants.

The model operates by rewarding individual users who contribute resources – such as bandwidth, storage capacity, or energy generation – with tokens, creating powerful incentives for participation. Blockchain technology ensures transparency and security, with decision-making distributed through decentralised governance mechanisms. Notable examples include the Helium Network, where individuals provide wireless coverage through hotspots and earn HNT tokens;

Filecoin, which enables users to rent out spare hard drive space for FIL tokens; and Energy Web Token, a platform facilitating peer-to-peer energy trading and grid management.

By building on digital economy primitives like tokens, smart contracts, and IoT devices, DePINs overcome traditional infrastructure limitations and the free-rider problem that often plagues public goods. This approach has the potential to disintermediate infrastructure provision, reducing both bureaucratic inefficiencies (the public sector curse) and rent-seeking activities (the private sector curse), while weakening infrastructure coalitions that can distort resource allocation in traditional models.

3.4.2 Quantum x Blockchain

Quantum Distributed Systems and Quantum Money

Quantum computing's impact remains highly uncertain but potentially revolutionary for specific computational tasks. Rohde (2021) explores how the quantum internet will enable combinatorial innovations by interconnecting quantum resources and systems across distributed networks. The key insight is that this quantum internet will drive a modular, distributed approach to quantum computation, similar to classical internet's distributed processing model. When quantum computers, communication networks, and cryptographic systems are combined, they unlock capabilities impossible for individual systems. For instance, interconnected quantum computers can distribute computation across nodes, exponentially amplifying capabilities as more qubits are integrated.

The high-level vision of the quantum internet is similar to that of the internet that has been built around classical computation but is enabled (and constrained) by radically different assumptions about what is being communicated and how. For example, the 'no cloning theorem' states that it is impossible to create an identical copy of an arbitrary unknown quantum state (Dieks 1982, Wootters and Zurek 1982). This theorem is a fundamental principle in quantum mechanics and quantum computing. Its implication is that arbitrary unknown quantum states cannot be replicated. As Cacciapuoti et al. (2019) write 'classical network functionalities are based on the assumption that classical information can be safely read and copied. However, this assumption does not hold in the Quantum Internet.'

The no-cloning characteristic of quantum information enables institutional innovations like quantum money – unforgeable 'notes' issued by financial institutions. In Weisner's scheme (1983, dating to 1970), physical bills would be encoded with randomly polarised photons, with banks retaining the randomisation data for verification. The no-cloning theorem would prevent counterfeiters from replicating the exact polarisation, addressing the double-spending problem that early digital cash work tackled (see also Lutomirski et al. 2009, Broadbent et al. 2024, Zhandry 2021). This quantum characteristic also enables other applications like private database queries (Giovannetti 2008, Lloyd 2009) and protecting privacy.

The history of classical distributed systems suggests a possible development of quantum distributed systems and the quantum internet. As Rohde notes, resource management is a critical factor in the development of quantum internet systems. One key solution is to introduce market mechanisms to coordinate resource use. We suggest that a mature quantum internet will require a quantum system of value and ownership, just as the classical internet now uses blockchain technology as an institutional technology to manage scarce and secure digital assets.

3.4.3 Zero Knowledge Proofs x Blockchain

Zero-knowledge proofs were first proposed in 1985 but have found their first major application in combination with blockchain technology, to solve one of the most complex problems that blockchains face: privacy. In the Bitcoin network, transactions are fully public and available on blockchain explorers, allowing any user to audit the complete history and verify legitimacy. While this transparency ensures network integrity, it compromises privacy. Although Bitcoin addresses aren't directly linked to identities, sophisticated observers can often connect addresses to individuals. Given the importance of financial privacy for autonomy and security (Berg 2018, Bailey et al. 2024), this transparency significantly limits Bitcoin's utility for privacy-conscious individuals and organisations requiring confidentiality.

The first major advancement in blockchain privacy came with ZCash in 2016, which introduced zero-knowledge proofs to conceal transaction details like addresses, amounts, and timing, while maintaining the trustworthiness of public blockchains. Based on the Zerocash protocol developed at Johns Hopkins University (Ben-Sasson et al. 2014), ZCash demonstrated how to create anonymous digital money. But while ZCash solved privacy for simple payments, the challenge of private programmable money remained unsolved.

This gap is now being addressed by projects like Penumbra, which extends privacy features beyond basic transactions to smart contracts and decentralised finance (De-Fi). Operating as a cross-chain network, Penumbra maintains ZCash's privacy guarantees for transaction data while enabling confidential interaction with smart contracts and network participation. This represents an evolution from private money to private programmable money, allowing users to engage in complex financial operations without compromising their privacy.

3.4.4 Low Earth Orbit Satellites x AI

Innovative hardware and software technology is building the LEO economy, which is lowering the cost of putting things in low earth orbit. The obvious things to put there are satellites, which are part robotic objects but mostly electronic relays. The benefit of those relays is that if you put enough of them up and can control the constellation, then you have a new economic information communications (i.e. compute and relay) infrastructure that is fast, cheap, and global first. And like the transport and communications infrastructure of the industrial economy – the roads, canals, sea lanes, ports, cable networks, railways, highways, and air corridors – the value of LEO compute and relays is not in themselves, but rather in the economic opportunities they create. LEO is capital infrastructure for a digital economy. And a key opportunity LEO creates is to expand the domain of things into which AI can be usefully and valuably integrated.

LEO expands the opportunity space for civilian AI integration at global scale. The commercial infrastructure of modern industrial economies *in general* supervened on what were initially, fundamentally, military technologies. The purpose of Roman roads was to defend and administer an empire. The strategic purpose of the construction and control of ports and rail networks was to facilitate naval blockade and troop movements. These military communications and logistics technologies are innovations and capital investments in the control of violence and creation of order that is a *necessary precondition* for large-scale economic cooperation (North et al. 2009). The internet was a military technology long before it was a commercial civilian technology (Greenstein 2017). Satellites were, and remain, a military technology that can be repurposed for commercial use. LEO somewhat follows this pattern, with strong and early support from, for example, defence contracting. But it also breaks with it in important ways, with powerful incentives to be inherently more open and permissionless owing to its global-first nature.

Another difference is that industrial transport and communications infrastructure primarily connects economic agglomerations to other agglomerations (cities to cities). These networks link industrial concentrations of activity due to external economies, as Alfred Marshall and Jane Jacobs explained, and are rationally supplied based on economic connection benefits (Batty 2013, Bettencourt 2013, Ortman et al. 2020). In contrast, LEO connects anything anywhere to everywhere, enabling a different spatial dynamic where operations can be controlled from any location. While surface infrastructure advances from specialisation and trade in urban centres, LEO drives automation into economic production beyond cities. It creates a new spatial economy by increasing returns to capital investment in rural and remote production through lower control and monitoring costs.

This transformation extends beyond traditional industries like agriculture, forestry, and mining. Any economic activity removed from cities, from tourism to ecological restoration, can now be informationally connected as if it were urban-based. LEO expands AI integration opportunities beyond complementary capital like factory automation and smart cities to the vast areas between population centres, potentially helping to reverse regional and rural decline.

3.4.5 IoT x Low Earth Orbit x Blockchain

We have seen that LEO and IoT can create both remote control and monitoring. With sufficiently advanced AI, monitoring autonomous machines (like mining drones or irrigation robots) becomes more feasible, likely driving investment in autonomous capital in remote economies. But we can also combine this remote monitoring capability (IoT x LEO) with trusted consensus (IoT x LEO x Blockchain) to create both new types of economic organisation and new types of capital. Rennie and Potts (2024) describe 'contribution systems' where groups coordinate individual efforts towards shared goals, benefiting proportionally to value created. While firms enable joint production through hierarchical monitoring and prior contracting, and commons-based production can be effective (Ostrom 1990, Kealey and Ricketts 2014), both have limitations, including high-powered incentives to contribute.

Rennie (2023) studied a new form of community production using digital technologies to achieve consensus around 'contributions' to projects. These systems use intersubjective consensus weighting to record and value contributions, creating monetary value over time. This enables open, permissionless joint production projects – from software development to ecological restoration – that maximise local knowledge and agency while integrating with the broader economy through objective value feedback. The system acts like a ledger entry in a project book, but one that dynamically records inputs and assesses their value based on their subsequent utilisation and development in a recursive manner.

Contribution systems compute over 'contributions' rather than market prices, converting novel objects into computable property rights by defining boundaries and properties. They can source information both endogenously (through self-reports and peer monitoring) and exogenously (via sensors, IoT devices, and satellites). This capability creates new forms of environmental resource management by creating high-powered incentives to regeneration and conservation by the management of ecological projects through contribution systems and the manufacture of new forms of 'ecological financial capital' made from these contributions that can then be used to finance further ecological investments (Potts et al. 2024).

3.5 How Combinatorics Evolves

In economics, there are conventionally two major explanations for growth and dynamics. The first is *investment*, which is delayed consumption, to build up capital stock (in all its forms), to increase productivity, to realise higher future consumption. Investment is intertemporal arbitrage. The second is *technological change*, which is also a type of investment in new knowledge, to increase the ability to transform resources into higher levels of consumption. 'Good institutions' are necessary to achieve either of those processes. Good institutions encourage savings and capital accumulation (sound money, efficient banking and finance, strong rule of law to protect property). And good institutions encourage innovation (McCloskey 2016, Mokyr 2016). Good institutions are good when they create high-powered incentives for socially beneficial behaviour. The fundamental importance of 'good institutions' as an explanation of long-run economic prosperity is one of the most robust findings in all of economics (Glaeser et al. 2004). But there is a third way to think about good institutions, which is that they increase the effective computational complexity of the world. They make more parts of the world into economic things.

Modern theory of economic growth distinguishes between two types of growth dynamics. The first was developed by Robert Solow in the 1950s and, using the so-called neoclassical production function, emphasises diminishing marginal productivity of investment. It predicts that without an exogenous source of ongoing technological change an economy will arrive at a stationary state of zero growth determined by its saving rate. In the 1980s and 1990s, economists such as Bob Lucas and Paul Romer developed new growth theory by endogenising the source of technological change with a new understanding of capital as knowledge that could feedback to create eleven further knowledge (formally, this was modelled by assuming capital was non-rivalrous and with spillovers). This was the same understanding that evolutionary economists such as Joseph Schumpeter and followers had long ago recognised. The upshot was an understanding of how an economy could grow (in principle) forever through innovation and technological change, or until it hit other exogenous constraints. Modern theories of economic growth therefore fundamentally recognise that knowledge builds on knowledge, that technologies are made of technologies, and because technology is combinatorial the process of economic growth by economic evolution works by exploiting this property of the universe.

If this theory is true, then we should be puzzled by observed 'secular stagnation', which is the seeming slow-down of the rates of growth in many modern economies (Eichengreen 2015, Summers 2016, Gordon 2018). There are many possible explanations for this phenomenon – from people simply choosing more leisure, adverse demographics and public investment, to high taxation and regulatory strangulation (i.e. increasing costs of innovation), to new ideas being more difficult to find. But our argument here is that in a type of Moore's Law for economic growth, where new large-scale breakthroughs must be made every so often to stay on the curve, the next huge leap in secular productivity growth will come from the supertransition.

While the productivity implications of the supertransition are not yet fully reflected in macroeconomic statistics, we have early evidence of large potential impacts. For instance, recent studies of generative AI adoption show substantial productivity gains – Brynjolfsson et al. (2023) found that customer service agents using AI assistance handled inquiries more effectively, while studies of GitHub Copilot showed a 26 per cent improvement in programmer productivity even with relatively early AI models (Cui et al. 2024). But there are important reasons why the full economic impact of these technologies may not yet be visible in aggregate productivity statistics. First, we are still in the early stages of the supertransition – while individual technologies like AI are showing promise, the combinatorial explosion of institutional possibilities is just beginning. Second, as Brynjolfsson et al. (2021) note, there is often a lag between the introduction of transformative technologies and their measured productivity benefits as complementary innovations and institutional adjustments take time to develop. Finally, standard productivity metrics may not fully capture the value created by new digital institutions, just as they struggled to measure the economic impact of earlier general purpose technologies during their early stages. The patterns we observe today – with clear micro-level productivity benefits but limited aggregate impact – are consistent with being at the start of a major technological and institutional transformation.

But how will this take-off in combinatorial innovation work? The supertransition is in play because all the technological trajectories are fundamentally digital, and so can interact and ramify. We have discussed that in the previous section, and through the examples earlier. That causes an explosion in the space of search, or in the possible niches that can exist, and therefore in the opportunities that can be discovered. GenerativeAI augmentation lowers the cost of that exploration, and spatial AI in devices enables increasing autonomy in things. LEO enables it to happen from anywhere on earth with low latency, which means safely and cheaply (Weinzierl 2023). Blockchains enable it to bypass failed states and low-capacity government administrations. And because many of these technologies are increasingly modular and distributed, meaning they can be installed on private devices such as phones and laptops, this empowers individuals, whomever and wherever they are. All of these forces mitigate against the industrial-era dominance of large-scale organisational planning and its trailing concentrations of power and profligate retail politics that eventually, but inevitably, stifles innovation and secular growth.

The supertransition is an opportunity to smooth out the corrugations and ravines cut by the wash of industrial-era institutional politics and policy. A digital economy is fundamentally supermodular and combinatorial in its innovation dynamics. In principle, because it is all information and computable, everything can connect with everything. That creates an explosion of combinatorial possibilities (Arthur 2009, Koppl et al. 2023). But a digital economy is also uniquely capable of institutional acceleration because those same properties also enable 'common knowledge' to spread – for things to know things about other things, and for those things to know that the other things know the things – and so to exploit the coordination opportunities that computation affords. This applies to object 'states' such as identity, location, ownership, property rights, exchange bids and asks, claims and promises, and all manner of possible information vectors under consensus as inputs into institutional coordination. The upshot of all this is the possibility of institutional acceleration.

4 Institutional Acceleration

In previous sections we explored how a specific cluster of new digital technologies is interacting and recombining in innovative new ways to produce new classes of economic goods and services and also, at the same time, new types of economic networks and systems. The existence and logic of this phenomenon is a major theme of this Element. The other major theme is the consequence of the supertransition, which forms the central prediction of this Element: that the dynamics driving this institutional technology supertransition are also *accelerating it*. In this section, we explore how institutions become technologies and how technological innovation then causes institutional acceleration. We define this new dynamic phenomenon and explore its consequences.

4.1 A Brief History of Institutional Technology

We are entering an era of institutional acceleration. The purpose of this section is to outline what this is, and to compare its logic to earlier forms of economic dynamics, such as capitalist economic growth and evolution, driven by entrepreneurial dynamics, industrial innovation, and technological trajectories. All of these forces have given rise to what we conjecture is a new phase of economic evolution shaped by institutional acceleration.

There is a tendency to valorise physical technologies because they are visible, as, for instance, in Stone Age, Iron Age, and Bronze Age artefacts in museums, or the age of iron and steam in beautiful Victorian-era buildings, bridges, or railways. In this view, the major technologies of the hominid species are things like fire, fish hooks, bow and arrow, sewing needles, plough, wheel, iron smelting, compass, steam engines, electricity, artificial fertilisers, internal combustion engines, telephone, vaccines, aeroplanes, plastics, semiconductors, rockets, and computers. Each of these major technological innovations[6] had enormous effects on the economy of the time. But there is another type of technology – institutions – that are historically just as significant but harder to see because where physical technologies transforming matter-energy, and thus leave clear evidence of their presence in the machinery of transformation or the effects, institutional technologies enable cooperation; that is, they cause economies to exist in the first place. Institutional technologies are among the oldest technologies to humanity (e.g. writing, numbers, legal code, names and administrative records, money) which originated in some of the earliest human civilisations, such as ancient Sumer, and long predate many modern physical technologies. New types of economies emerge with new institutional technologies. We can see this in history, marking phases and transitions. Innovation in new technologies of institutions is the origin of all economies and explains the history of economies.

This argument is well made by economic historians and institutional economists. North and Thomas (1973) and North (1981) explain how the origin of modern capitalism, as the transition from the feudal order prior to the fourteenth century and culminating in the industrial revolution of the eighteenth century was fundamentally an institutional transition in technologies of property rights, factory systems, and markets, or, as Allen (2011) describes it, an institutional revolution.[7] And the argument is also well supported in related fields such as evolutionary anthropology. Henrich (2020) traces the eleventh-century institutional revolutions in the Catholic church, from a ban on cousin marriage to its long-range consequence on property rights. Graeber and Wengrow (2021) map differential selection on institutions in prehistory to the types of economies that exist now. Historians such as Karl Jaspers (1948) long ago theorised how the simultaneous invention of philosophy in many parts of the world during the 'axial age' created the intellectual conditions for new types of writing-based economies to emerge.

---

[6] What Joseph Schumpeter called *technological waves*, and what evolutionary economists following him called *technological trajectories*, or what Joel Mokyr calls *macro-inventions*.

[7] For broader historical context, see Williamson (2000); North, Wallis, and Weingast (2009).

So ours is certainly not a novel thesis. What is new is the technological embodiment of institutions and the new affordances this creates. This is an argument we have previously made in a subfield we called *institutional cryptoeconomics* (Berg et al. 2019, Allen et al. 2020) in relation to blockchain technology. But our claim, as stated earlier, is that a recent cluster of advanced digital technologies is driving transformative innovation in new internet-native digital money, digital identity, digital registries, digital exchanges, digital assets, digital contracts, digital organisations, and so on.

4.2 Institutions Are Technologies

4.2.1 Institutions Enable Economic Computation

In economic theory, institutions are defined as the 'rules of the game in a society'.

> Institutions are the humanly devised constraints that structure political, economic, and social interaction. They consist of both informal constraints (sanctions, taboos, customs, traditions, and codes of conduct), and formal rules (constitutions, laws, property rights). (North 1991: 97)

> Institutions form the incentive structure of a society, and the political and economic institutions, in consequence, are the underlying determinants of economic performance. . . . Institutions and the technology employed determine the transaction and transformation costs that add up to the costs of production. (North 1994: 359)

North emphasises that these rules are both constraints and incentives, which is how institutions work to coordinate groups of humans. But institutions, as rules, are also a form of cooperation and common knowledge, in that we each know that these rules also apply to others, and that others know they apply to us, and so their behaviours become somewhat predictable, which enables complex social coordination by following institutional rules. When these rule-systems work well, institutions function as a kind of social operating system (in the computer science sense of a shared code-base) for economic computation of value. The model of an economy as a giant distributed rule-governed information processing system (i.e. a computer) was first elaborated by Hayek (1945) in his account of the role of the price mechanism in the market process.[8] But the broader insight was developed in the so-called socialist calculation debates.

> Human cooperation under the system of the social division of labor is possible only in the market economy. Socialism is not a realizable system of society's

---

[8] See Mirowski (2001) for a general historical account of the rise of the metaphor of the computer in modern economics, especially in game theory.

economic organization because it lacks any method of economic calculation. (Mises 1949: 679)

Hayek argued that the market mechanism was an ingenious device – a complex social technology not invented by anyone, but rather that had evolved – that acted to gather and process distributed 'local information' and compute them into 'prices'. These computed price signals – as outputs of the market computation – then worked to efficiently and effectively guide economic activity at scale. The price system, which is built on institutions of private property, market mechanisms, profit and loss accounting, is a rule-governed process of economic computation. Market mechanisms are distributed mechanisms that perform complex *economic computation* on knowledge, information, and resources. In this view, an economy is clearly a type of computer.

The concept of a computable number (or Turing machine) is a useful way to think about the meaning of a 'digital economy' as a 'computable economy'. Just as computable and non-computable numbers exist, the corollary is that so do computable and non-computable economies. An economy is computable in the same way, namely there exists a set of rules (i.e. institutions, technologies) that generates economic output as a finite set of operations. Analogously, a fully computable economy is a 'Turing complete economy'. A computable economy is one where economic action (i.e. transactions) can be digitally connected as part of an algorithmic process. A 'Turing complete economy' is one where all economic actions can be digitally constructed and implemented. A *computable economy* is one in which those computational rule systems are joined up into a connected graph, and thus have a form of completeness (i.e. all parts are 'computable'). The evolutionary process by which all parts become computable is the basic logic of the digital economy revolution.

4.2.2 What Are Institutional Technologies?

So institutions are rule systems in use that enable cooperation over a population of agents and produce economic computation. They are a kind of 'social technology' that performs 'economic computation'. But these institutions will be variously embodied in different types of physical technology objects that human subjects (economic agents) interact with. Which is to say that the rules are technologically embodied, and are therefore subject to technological innovation and change. In this way, institutions can technologically evolve in the substrate through which they are operationalised. As such, institutional rules can change in their semantic content of the rule (i.e. its meaning), but they can also change in the way it is embodied and operationalised. Institutional technologies are the rules and institutions and their material embodiments that facilitate economic coordination (administrative ledgers, market mechanisms, consensus mechanisms, oracles, voting mechanisms, digital money and identity, dispute resolution mechanisms, etc.). As a simple example, records of ownership of an asset, which must be updated when a transaction occurs, can be embodied in a book made of paper and cardboard, or can be embodied in a digital database. And that database can be centralised, or distributed. It can be protected with a firewall encryption, or with consensus algorithms. The same institutional rules (e.g. for updating an asset registry) can be built with very different technologies, which in turn have very different costs and functional properties (speed, legibility, security, fault tolerance, etc.).

Deep evolution in the technologies of the industrial economy has in turn led to specific evolution of institutional technologies. An industrial economy, of the sort that began with the industrial revolution in the early 1800s and gradually spread around the world in the subsequent centuries, is composed of *industrial production* technologies and the resources they create – such as steam power, iron and steel, minerals, engines, trucks, rockets, oil, synthetic materials, petrochemicals, pharmaceuticals, electrification, railways, satellites, transistors, lasers, computers, microelectronics, and ICT. When most economists think of technological change and innovation, it is change in these things (e.g. Freeman and Soete 1997).

An industrial economy also refers to *industrial institutions*. These include the factory system and private corporations, industrial sectors, industry policy, venture finance, public economic institutions to support markets, for example, money, banks, property registries (including IPR), courts, regulation, roads, ports, and universities. These are modernist administrative technologies of government (Scott 1999). For hundreds of years previous, the origin of economic order – the supply of these institutions – came from government (North and Thomas 1973, North 1982) and from corporations. These were analogue and centralised institutions, although by the late twentieth century due to the mass adoption of ICT, some had become computerised. This occurred both in the private sector (e.g. telecommunications, banking, airline bookings) and, more slowly, in the public sector (e.g. identity, land registry, tax collection). The major transition in the world today is to digital institutions which have very recently become composable, modular, and able to be combined quickly and easily in new ways to build new economic institutions and organisations.

4.2.3 A Digital Economy Means Digital Institutions

Industrial economies have profoundly changed the global history of humanity. The major, epoch-defining technological breakthrough that enables institutional acceleration began with the innovation trajectory of digital technologies.

Modern computers are all digital, which goes back to Claude Shannon's 1948 insight that digital signals could represent logical (Boolean) operators, which enabled a path from electricity to circuits to semantics.[9] Digital means that rule systems can be computational. And that means two things.

The first is *software*, which is putting rules into things wherever things can be made digital. This is often what people think of when they think of a digital economy, namely all the things (economic goods, devices, objects, machines, etc. that are now programmable) that are now digital and how they are everywhere in the economy. And this explosion of digital goods and services, of the growth of ICT and digital industries, has indeed been revolutionary and transformative. But that digital goods and services – computers everywhere – is the surface level of the digital economy.

The second is *digital institutions*, when that software (and hardware) is the basis of economic coordination. This is a deep-level transformation to a digital economy, and is the fundamental shift we emphasise here as the driver of institutional acceleration. That is, the digital economy revolution specifically refers to the disruption and regrowth of *analogue economic institutions in digital format*. The industrial economy is the proximate cause of the digital economy revolution, by advancing innovation and indeed industrial mass production of digital technology. But the epochal transition from an *industrial economy* to a *digital economy*, which is the specific significance of the cryptoeconomy, is a consequence of the transformation of industrial economic institutions (money, identity, contracts, registries, and economic organisation, coordination and governance in general) into natively digital institutions. The result is a 'full stack' digital economy. The cluster of digital technologies and their combinatorics, then, is a compounding force that is driving computation deep into the economy. The essential nature of a digital economy is not digital goods and services, or investment in digital industries or sectors, but rather a large-scale transformation in economic institutions (i.e. the technologies that coordinate people and machines to create economic value) to be fundamentally digital. A true digital economy is digital in its institutions. This transition enables an economic order to be vastly more natively computable and complex.

The reason this deep digital transformation is significant on the historical timeline is because it enables an order of magnitude shift in the computational capacity of economic institutions, and in the connective reach of economic institutions. Anything digital can, in principle (conditional upon interface standards), interact with anything else digital. This means that digital economic

---

[9] www.technologyreview.com/2001/07/01/235669/claude-shannon-reluctant-father-of-the-digital-age/.

institutions can potentially scale very quickly and cheaply, potentially to global scale, and can, if appropriately designed, operate in an open and permissionless manner. Economic institutions compute, new technologically evolved digital institutions compute better, faster and cheaper, and can reach much greater scale and efficiency.

4.3 Constraints on Institutional Evolution

Institutional acceleration is surprising because the 'natural state' of an institution is at rest, as a stable point or the equilibrium of a game. Many institutions are conventions, or norms and customs, which are rules that are well known, and which have evolved under evolutionary selection, and that are constituted by behaviours that in turn produce patterns of expected outcomes and predictable behavioural responses (Heiner 1983, Aoki 2007). Institutions have a kind of behavioural and cultural 'inertial mass' that makes them both persistent and difficult to change. But that property, which is largely emergent, can also be understood as a rational investment (by an institutional designer) such that a 'good institution' has positive social and economic properties in lowering transaction costs and shaping economic incentives towards the creation of cooperation and wealth (e.g. North and Thomas 1973). As such, a rational institutional designer would create good institutions that are also costly to create (to raise the cost of creating competing institutions) and also costly to change (to raise the cost of those seeking to modify institutions for their own benefit.

Researchers and scholars in the fields of political economy and public choice theory have long emphasised the role and importance of public order and governance systems, including strong constitutions, bicameral parliamentary systems, independent courts, public control of the military, and rule of law (Buchanan and Tullock 1962, North et al. 2009). These complex political and legal systems (i.e. nation states) are found worthy due to their properties of distributive justice, incentive compatibility with human rights, the delivery of public goods, and the production of wealth and prosperity, and their costliness in construction and process is justified in these terms. But the costliness is also part of the point, in that while nation building is difficult and expensive, these investments also make these institutions more resistant to change and especially to disorder and decay.

But the inverse of this property is that institutions built this way are also hard to innovate over. In this respect they are unlike most other 'technologies' where rapid change and innovation is a good property. Institutions do, of course, change through both designed and evolutionary processes, but these tend to be slow-moving, and so are generally treated as parameters in most economic and social contexts as they change slowly in historical time, including evolution of culture (Hayek 1960), or that change was deliberate (i.e. political reform). The idea of institutional technologies and the prospect of institutional acceleration is a new way of thinking about economic and social dynamics.

4.3.1 Jurisdictions for Institutional Experimentation

The supertransition thesis hinges on the accelerating pace of institutional evolution. Historically, institutional change has been slow, constrained by jurisdiction-based rules that result in path dependence, regulatory capture, and entrenched interests. These constraints have limited institutional diversity and experimentation. The technologies driving institutional acceleration act as catalysts by enabling arbitrage around these constraints, pushing us towards more open, complex, and permissionless institutional evolution.

Many of our institutions are jurisdiction-based, with the institutional context for trade, coordination, and cooperation determined by the nation-state or jurisdiction in which we physically reside or are domiciled. This structure has benefits, such as reduced transaction costs when trading with physical neighbours and a default institutional set that reduces decision-making costs. But constraining institutions to geographical jurisdictions also creates frictions, such as transaction costs in regional or global trading relationships. International bodies have emerged to harmonise these costs through agreements and mutual recognition. Because the number of jurisdictions is relatively stable we end up with a stable and capped number of institutional types, as well as institutions that tailor to minimum-viable groups of people, rather than enabling more bespoke institutional matching. We lack institutional diversity.

Jurisdictions also suppress some competitive dynamics in institutional evolution. While competition exists within liberal democratic orders and across borders in federated systems, substantial frictions remain in the flow of capital, organisations, and people across those boundaries. These cross-jurisdictional flows have led to some specialisation (e.g. tax havens), but they still limit the potential for institutional evolution propelled by competition. A fixed set of jurisdiction-based institutions also reduces institutional experimentation. While mechanisms for institutional change exist, experimenting with new institutions, especially those that radically alter the institutional design space, is often prohibitively costly. One of the reasons they are costly is because of the entrenched interests that build up in our existing institutions.

4.3.2 Entrenched Interests Constraining Institutional Evolution

Rather than some romantic view of politics, public choice theorists have long studied politics as exchange. In their seminal book *The Calculus of Consent*, political economists Buchanan and Tullock (1962) view political processes as transactions, where politicians, bureaucrats, and interest groups exchange regulatory favours for political support. As Stigler (1971) noted, regulators can become captured by industry: 'as a rule, regulation is acquired by the industry and is designed and operated primarily for its benefit.' One classic example of this is the 'bootleggers and baptists' phenomenon described by Bruce Yandle, where seemingly opposed groups (e.g. bootleggers and temperance advocates) support the same regulations (e.g. Sunday alcohol sales bans) for different reasons. This coalition-forming creates barriers to institutional evolution.

Our argument is that technological combinatorics not only necessitates institutional evolution but will also propel institutional acceleration because they enable institutional experimentation and arbitrage. Entrepreneurs can use tools such as blockchains and artificial intelligence to bypass traditional jurisdictional constraints and challenge entrenched interests. They lower the costs of institutional experimentation, increase the potential for institutional arbitrage, and create new competitive pressures on existing institutions. As we will see in Section 5, this leads us towards a more open, complex, global(ist), distributed, and liberal digital economy. This technological-driven institutional acceleration forms the core of the supertransition.

4.3.3 Property Rights

How are institutional constraints overcome? The common answer is through politics. But that is slow, costly, and often corrupt, or at least with poor incentives, as public choice theory and political economy teaches. A better way is through institutional innovation. The mechanism through which this specifically occurs is often property rights. New technologies enable citizens to overcome constraints to institutions.

Property rights define the basic connection between objects (i.e. resources) in an economy and subjects (i.e. people, agents) who make economic operations (i.e. production and exchange). The rules by which subjects interact are institutions, and property rights define the content of those object-oriented actions. The structure of property rights determines transaction costs of different forms of economic organisation and institutions, which in turn shape the overall structure of economic activity. When property rights are given, we can ignore them to focus on fast-changing variables (e.g. prices). Property rights are mostly created and enforced by government, so are a proxy for state capacity, or level of development. As such, economic explanations based on property rights tend to be the province of economic historians or comparative development (e.g. North and Thomas 1973, Acemoglu and Robinson 2012). New digital technologies (such as tokenisation and smart contracts) are significantly expanding the set of objects in an economy that can be connected into rule systems.

The revolution that digital brings is an explosion in the number and types of things over which property rights can be attached, and so a massive expansion in the institutional design space of economies. Digital makes property rights and institutions fast-changing economic variables. The digital revolution enhances and expands property rights. Blockchains exemplify this integration by merging the object (token) with the property rights enforcement system (protocol). By expanding property rights and designing new incentive mechanisms, digital institutions create a more efficient and adaptable economic system.

4.4 Institutional Acceleration

Institutional acceleration is a process of innovation in institutions (and property rights) happening as economic agents adopt and use these digital representations of economic institutions, and it is accelerating, which is to say that there are feedback processes at work driving increasing returns. The cause of the acceleration is combinatorial explosion and recombination of digital technologies. Digital technologies are a lingua franca – anything digital can talk to anything else digital, forming a common language across which all can in principle interact. This then leverages benefits from modular and composable designs and architectures at the level of institutions. Institutional elements can function like open-source software that can be mixed and reused. The idea of technological recombination as an evolutionary process is not new, and traces back to a theoretical model of a continuously expanding economy developed by the legendary mathematician John von Neumann in 1932 (but published in 1945). Modern versions of the same underlying intuition about the sources of long-run economic growth and economic dynamics are found in Kauffman's (1993) NK model, Potts' (2000) growth theoretic model of economic evolution, and Arthur's (2009) general theory of technological combinatorics (see Schrepel 2024). Koppl et al.'s (2023) 'Theory of the Adjacent Possible' model is a parsimonious modern synthesis of these ideas.

Institutional change and innovation is a new way of thinking about economic dynamics. Institutional acceleration is recognition that not only can institutions change, but that the process of accelerating institutional change *is the thing creating new economic opportunities* (including growth, flourishing, wealth, etc.). Institutional acceleration is therefore one of the most surprising dynamic forces in the world today. And it will radically reshape what our economy of digital institutions looks like.

5 An Economy of Digital Institutions

What type of economy does institutional acceleration and the supertransition build? What are the core economic concepts we should use to think about this? We argue that digital economies built by the technologies of the supertransition are open, complex, global, and distributed. These are the fundamental properties and qualities of the new institutional order. We also recognise that data is a new resource, and the challenge is its institutional representation. This section will explain why these properties are important and good in the context of the supertransition. These are the essential institutional characteristics of the new i/acc world. We will use these core concepts to think about what to do – that is, strategy – in Section 6 to follow.

5.1 Open

Today's technology rhetoric focuses on the dominance of large technology companies such as the FAANGs (Facebook, Amazon, Apple, Netflix, and Google). Many of these businesses do operate as multi-sided markets with complex payment structures and subsidies, where consumers have little control over their data and their networks. Barriers are intentionally raised to increase switching costs (such as moving to competitors). It's no wonder that people view technology as a force for closure. Given the current trajectory of the digital economy, a crucial question is raised: Will the supertransition create an economy with greater openness or increasing closure?

Contrary to the trend towards large closed platforms in the early stages of the digital economy, we argue that the supertransition is propelling us towards a more open economy. More open institutions will enable people and objects to move freely across the boundaries of organisations, ecosystems, and jurisdictions. Two key factors drive this more open digital economy. First, many of the technology vectors we have described, such as blockchains and open-source AI models, are already trending towards openness. And, second, the principle of combinatorics thrives on openness. The more open segments of the economy, and parts of the technology, will likely experience faster institutional acceleration.

Despite the slipperiness of the concept, we need a working definition of openness. In the content of institutions (i.e. rule systems) openness implies permeable boundaries, unrestricted access, and a lack of confining barriers. It represents a 'non-gated' approach where individuals have the freedom to make decisions about digital assets or organisations without external constraints. Openness is also associated with visibility and searchability (or at least variability), empowering individuals to make informed decisions and to coordinate.

Open manifests in different ways in various parts of the economy. In academic publishing, open is open *access* – enabling ideas to combine. Between jurisdictions, open is open *trade* – reducing the barriers to new patterns of specialisation and trade. In software, open is open-*source* – enabling developers to use, reuse, and mix code to suit their applications. For organisations, open can mean *open innovation* – seeing ideas from outside the boundaries of the firm, rather than relying on internal resources and ideas.

One way to understand open institutions is in contrast to closed institutions. Closed institutional systems are more familiar, operating with restricted access, opaque boundaries, limited external visibility, and barriers to entry. A typical hierarchical firm is closed, with a boundary, and some defined resources inside and outside of that closed system. Nation states and jurisdictions also implement 'closed' in different ways – through immigration restrictions, capital controls, voting rights, and restrictions on launching new businesses and ideas through legislative constraints.

The choice between open and closed systems involves significant trade-offs – open and closed institutions are usefully understood as two ends of an institutional spectrum. Open systems, while facilitating innovation and adaptability, present challenges in developing sustainable business models due to fewer control points and increased competition (openness means open to your competitors, too). At the other end of the spectrum, closed institutional systems provide protection for resources and business models, and are effective at executing defined plans and keeping secrets. But closed systems struggle to rapidly evolve to changing environmental conditions and accessing resources outside their boundaries, sometimes limiting innovation. While closed systems provide protection, their closed nature limits interactions, and hence combinatorics.

There are two main drivers of the openness of the digital economy, where objects and assets can move more freely across boundaries. First, many of the technology vectors we have described earlier are already trending towards openness. ZKPs facilitate increased cross-organisational trade by mitigating privacy-related costs. Blockchain-based digital assets enable the seamless transfer of value and property rights across traditional organisational boundaries. Applications of blockchains to create autonomous economic agents will thrive in more open environments because it expands their capacity to trade and act agentically. Open-source AI models are challenging the dominance of closed, proprietary systems.

Second, openness enables combinatorics. More open parts of the economy will institutionally accelerate faster than closed parts of the economy. Combinatorics requires different technologies and organisations to combine in novel ways, which enables the passing of knowledge and value across organisations. Open expands the design space for institutional innovation. The combinatorial power of open-source software is well known. Developers can freely access, modify, and redistribute code, leading to rapid iterations and novel applications. We can also apply this principle more broadly across the technological vectors we have described, propelling a process of combinatorics. Openness, when powered up across multiple technological vectors, can dramatically expand the possibilities for institutional innovation in the digital economy.

The supertransition not only predicts but also necessitates increasingly open technologies and digital institutions. Openness is desirable for many reasons. It enables people (and machines) to make choice, including choices that facilitate emergent order and self-organisation. More open institutions use the local knowledge of particular circumstances of time and choice to be put to use through an institutional system. Openness can also destroy accumulated rents in closed institutional systems (North et al. 2009).

Openness is a catalyst for institutional acceleration by enabling new technological combinations, but it also requires deliberate choices to maintain. Institutions provide the context within which we apply technologies, including a culture of entrepreneurship and process, but those technologies can also be used to build new types of institutions, through the institutional acceleration we have described earlier. In this section we have emphasised open institutions, and we have made the claim that the forces of the supertransition will propel us towards openness. The evolution towards open institutions requires conscious effort and design, balancing the benefits of openness with the challenges it presents.

Open economies do not exist in a natural state – they require deliberate institutional design. While we can imagine a primordial, open world free from formalised institutions like nation-states and property rights, such openness alone did not foster the specialisation and trade patterns crucial for prosperity. The development of complex economies necessitated new institutions to facilitate trade and coordination.

Institutional design evolves through experimentation over time. Millennia of institutional evolution, from feudalism to market capitalism, have revealed different costs of these institutional systems. Scholars have identified key institutional characteristics that promote innovation and growth. Acemoglu and Robinson (2012: 74) identify desirable institutions that are 'inclusive', including those that 'feature secure private property' and 'permit the entry of new businesses'. Mokyr (2016) emphasised an informal culture that valued knowledge, innovation, and intellectual exchange as a critical feature of sustained economic growth and prosperity during the Industrial Revolution. Other scholars, such as McCloskey (2006, 2016), have pinpointed the development of bourgeois virtues, such as trust and responsibility, as a driver of the great enrichment.

But there are also forces that tend institutions to become closed over time, including regulatory capture and the preservation of economic rents. Public choice theory suggests that closed institutions develop path dependencies due to vested interests resisting change. Counteracting this trend, various movements advocate for openness, particularly in areas like intellectual property law. The free software and copyleft movements exemplify this push against institutional capture. Open movements have focused on open institutions through copyright and intellectual property law, such as the copyleft or free software movements – which are pushing back on the tendency for capture into closed systems (Stallman 2002). The institutional accelerationism (i/acc) that we lay out in the final section is fundamentally an open movement.

Today's challenge is in designing institutions that are more open and facilitate trade, such as clear property rights, while also enabling porous boundaries necessary for combinatorial innovation. Both private and public institutions have evolved to create systems of openness, enabling more open markets including trading of goods and services with lower transaction costs and in more complex ways. Groups can come together to create common property regimes that create collectively governed common resources (Ostrom 1990). The institutional acceleration we have described throughout this Element represents a similar shift towards new more open institutional systems that foster both openness and complexity. For now we turn to why the digital economy will not only be more open, but it will also be more complex.

5.2 Complex

The economy after the supertransition will be more complex. But in what way? The most obvious way that the economy will be more complex is the familiar march of technological complexity. Technologies are not merely tools – they are embodiments of knowledge that can be combined and recombined in novel ways (Arthur 2009). Each technology represents a crystallisation of human understanding and problem-solving. When these technologies are combined, their embedded knowledge interacts in unpredictable ways, creating new capabilities that are more than the sum of their parts. Our argument here is that this technological complexity enables more important institutional and economic complexity – which drives more coordination and compute into our societies, enabling more growth and prosperity.

We are moving into a radically expanded design space of digital institutions. Not only are we seeing technological complexity, but that is feeding into more institutional complexity. More open digital institutions, and more experimentation with them, means a more complex institutional environment. There is far more institutional diversity beyond the dichotomy of markets and states (Ostrom 2005). Indeed, there is a long history of communities building private complex institutions to solve coordination problems, often outside of the eyes of the state (Scott 1999, Leeson 2014, Stringham 2015). We now have technological combinatorics enabling a process of institutional experimentation. New institutional types become possible. Traditional hierarchies are being complemented and sometimes replaced by DAOs and other hybrid structures that blur the lines between firms, markets, and networks. For instance, rather than institutions being defined by the jurisdiction that we live in, such as public infrastructure networks, we'll see more private digital infrastructure networks emerge through the combination of LEO and blockchains.

At first, institutional complexity sounds bad. Modern developed industrial economies periodically and legitimately seek to create simpler institutions, whether as political acts of deregulation or as administrative acts of reducing costs and confusion for citizens, and within which innovation and entrepreneurship could flourish. But part of that desire for institutional simplicity was because of the way institutions were jurisdictionally tied – they had to be simple to enable many people to operate under the same rules. A broad church. But digital institutions through the supertransition alter the calculus of institutional complexity: we can have more institutional complexity because we can have open, global, and overlapping institutions. It's not that any one individual or organisation needs to operate under complex rules, it's that they have a broader space of choice in how they coordinate and govern their activities. This works if there are more opportunities for institutional exit – the ability to opt out of one system and into another. Exit serves as a powerful force for institutional evolution and improvement.

Of course, institutional complexity is not valuable in itself, but is a means to the end of *economic complexity*. Institutions are the rules of the game that lower transaction costs and enable us to coordinate and trade. When institutions are better matched to us then we can drive down transaction costs and enable more coordination. It is not surprising that economic complexity is a strong predictor of economic growth and prosperity (Hidalgo 2015). We can see this push towards deeper economic complexity in our expanding options for monies, contracts, identities online. We can also see if in efforts to create movements such as network states (Srinivasan 2022) and non-territorial jurisdictions (MacDonald 2019). But through institutional combinatorics we predict even more choices in infrastructure, from autonomous agents to decentralised private infrastructure networks. More diverse and sophisticated patterns of specialisation and trade make a more computable economy.

5.3 Global

A powerful and disruptive property of the supertransition – and the institutional acceleration it brings – is that it builds new economies 'global first'. By new economies, we mean the economic coordination infrastructure that digital institutions assemble, usually in the form of protocol layers, and that enables a group of people to work together and interact productively (possibly anonymously, without central coordination, from anywhere on earth). The origins of this technical possibility trace back to the early twentieth century with the emergence of private order communication networks (such as Ham radio and citizen band radio communications, Haring 2007) and that evolved into the cultural foundations of the early internet and open-source software (Turner 2006, Rid 2016, Tozzi 2017, Nabban 2023). These networks were culturally open but they were also *geographically open* due to the long-range signal broadcasting capabilities of radio, and then the gradual weaving of terrestrial and then satellite telecommunications networks. With open access network standards, the internet and the World Wide Web are with some important exceptions; for example, national firewalls are global economic information and communications infrastructure. Economic institutions that are engineered to run primarily or even entirely on this protocol and transport layer are global first.

The supertransition pushes us towards more globally accessible digital institutions and trade, and therefore into a more globalised and globalist world. We're moving into a post-jurisdictional environment, with fewer institutions tied to the legislative creation prospects, regulatory governance, and in enforcement capabilities of nation states. But also into a world in which new governing institutions – often as platforms and protocols – are emerging, and often global first. Multinational corporations have long provided effective mechanisms to deliver economic institutions at global scale, and do so in partnership with particular countries, as the basis of regulatory compliance and taxation, in return for legal protection (Davidson et al. 2020). But cryptographically secured distributed consensus digital protocols enable economic institutions to supply their own security and order, shifting the margin of competition with nation states in the supply of economic infrastructure. Now, these new protocols are both better and worse. On some margins, such as cost and speed, internet-based digital infrastructure is superior to modern economy nation states. But on other margins, such as deep integration with legal systems, military force capabilities and political systems, even advanced digital protocols are inferior. Potts (2024), for instance, characterises layer 1 blockchains as 'limited access orders' in the North et al. (2009) framework of long-run social and economic evolution. Yet either way, the supertransition is bringing competition to the supply of economic infrastructure (Teece 2012, 2018).

Institutional acceleration is happening at a global-first scale because the hardware and physical infrastructure required for this is now, finally, globally installed and operating cheaply and efficiently. The internet, for instance, is not a single global network, but a network of networks made possible by interoperability standards but that relays across interconnected and extremely complex telecommunications backhaul networks (made of wire, fibre, microwaves, and satellites, forming the world's biggest machine) that have been evolving since the nineteenth century (Leiner et al. 2003). There are now billions of devices everywhere on earth, almost everyone has one, and they are nearly all connected. Digital communication at global scale is one of the greatest triumphs of the industrial era. Some see it as a universal human right. But it is the foundation of global-first innovation in economic institutions.

Global-first is good because it advances liberty, enabling in principle anyone anywhere access to high-quality economic institutions through the internet. Competition induces innovation. It is also good because that same process provides competition to existing institutions. Competition disciplines poor behaviour. Nation state governments have less ability to prey on their citizens if those citizens have viable exit options in the economic institutions they use (MacDonald 2019, Srinivasan 2022).

5.4 Distributed and Decentralised

An institutionally accelerated digital economy also has the property of being more distributed and decentralised. A centralised system is one in which all information, or compute or decision-making, passes through a single (central) node. In an organism, think of this node as the brain. In an organisation, think of it as the boss or leader. Centralisation brings powerful efficiencies to decision-making, ensuring all information is processed through a single point. But this architecture also creates critical vulnerabilities and chokepoints for information flow. Centralised systems are hard to scale, lack security and robustness, and make poor use of local information.

In certain types of environments, systems may evolve away from being centralised to improve functional fitness by becoming more *distributed* and *decentralised*, in which decision-making occurs over multiple nodes. This approach is more expensive, but also much more secure and fault tolerant, and therefore more robust. While an economy with highly centralised institutions can make, in principle, well-coordinated plans, it struggles with large, complex, local, or changing information, and so will tend to perform poorly in open, complex, or dynamic environments. In contrast, an economy with more decentralised institutions will be better adapted to a more dynamic economic environment.

This insight into complex systems was well elaborated by Simon (1968) and Hayek (1960). But it is also foundational in computer science. Joseph Weizenbaum, the inventor of the 1964 project ELIZA – one of the earliest attempts at a building a natural language computer interface chatbot and a descendent of our modern ChatGPT – argued in 1985 that computers had been 'a fundamentally conservative force' that preserved existing institutions which 'which otherwise might have had to be changed'. The computer enabled big business to scale management and handle increasing information complexity and 'solidified power where it already existed' (Ben-Aaron 1985). The growth of global corporations relied heavily on digital information management tools (Cortada 2011). Back-office technologies like relational databases and spreadsheets are the foundations of the large multinational companies. Likewise, the modern state runs on the computer (Agar 2003). But Weizenbaum was speaking before the internet, a radically decentralising force that expanded free speech and disrupted the staid media environment of the twentieth century.

This principle now extends to governing institutions, which for most of human history have been centrally supplied by powerful governments or other large hierarchical organisations (Hodgson 2015) but are now increasingly supplied by the commons (Potts 2019, Murtazashvili et al. 2022). The institutional acceleration is the era in which private order institutions, which are inherently distributed and decentralised, can on some important margins begin to compete with centralised economic institutions (Frolov 2021, Alston et al. 2022).

5.5 Data and Property Rights

Open, complex, global, and decentralised are all adaptive properties of economies built by the supertransition. But a further property to consider are the new resources that such economies build. There are two that we want to emphasise.

One – data – is relatively well understood as a new type of resource in a digital economy, but the other – property rights – is more surprising due to how they are originating from the affordances of the supertransition, in consensus agreement about data over the explosion of new objects in the digital economy.

Property rights are the foundation of any economy. They define the basic connection between objects (i.e. resources) in an economy and subjects (i.e. people, agents) who make economic operations (i.e. production and exchange). The rules by which subjects interact are institutions and property rights define the content of those object-oriented actions. The structure of property rights determines transaction costs of different forms of economic organisation and institutions, which in turn shapes the overall structure of economic activity.

When property rights are assumed given and unchanging, as in many practical situations, economists can safely ignore them to instead focus on fast-changing economic variables such as quantities and prices. Property rights are mostly created and enforced by the government, and a proxy for state capacity, quality, or level of development. As such, economic explanations based on property rights tend to be the province of economic historians or comparative development (e.g. Schumpeter 1942, North and Thomas 1973, Allen 2011, Acemoglu and Robinson 2012). But digital technologies enable private actors to create new forms of property rights by attaching data to objects with consensus (Harper 2013).

Institutional acceleration is significantly expanding the set of objects in an economy that can be connected into rule systems. The clearest example is tokenisation and smart contracts, which is a form of property right that is automatically self-enforcing. The benefit is low transaction costs and high scalability in space and time. The revolution that digital brings is an explosion in the number and types of things over which property rights can be attached, and so a massive expansion in the institutional design space of economies. Digital makes property rights and institutions fast-changing economic variables.

Data is the most important new economic resource in the world and a direct consequence of digital technologies (Coyle et al. 2020, Jones and Tonetti 2020). The supertransition will fundamentally shape how that value is realised and distributed due to a profound shift in the institutions governing data. Data is an input to economic production. The base layer is administrative data (i.e. identity, address, etc.) that is collected by the state and required for delivery of public services and to track obligations (e.g. taxes). Public administration data sets pertaining to citizenry are mostly legislated monopolies. Almost all economic exchanges involve the co-production of data, meaning the consumer and producer are both involved in its creation, and so it is difficult to establish clear and well-delineated ownership. In consequence, data markets mostly fail due to weak and unclear property rights – for example, costliness in establishing, attaching, verifying and enforcing property rights; search costs and missing markets. Data is also by definition a non-standard good, and usually only valuable when aggregated or triangulated (i.e. used with other data).

So, can new technologies be used to create better property rights in data? All platform businesses (from search engines to exchanges and now AI platforms) collect data, and that data is held by the firm and used in order to deliver services. Who owns it? Where do the property rights go? The growth of the digital platform economy (Goldfarb and Tucker 2019) has driven public attention and legislation to ensure that citizen welfare reflects the value of that data, and is commensurate with the risks involved in producing and sharing it. Over-collected data is inevitable in platform contexts, and includes things like the time of an inquiry, or geolocation, or type of platform accessed from, and so on. This is a type of 'midden heap' of data (or by-catch, to use a factory fishing metaphor) that the business might not even be aware that it has collected. The upshot is that populist legislative constraints on data use in core business can inadvertently work to increase the security of the residual data the firm has collected, as it has in effect been tested in court. As new legislation such as GDPR and the EU's digital data act have sought to clarify these rights, as to what data firms are able to use, and what remains under control of users, the property rights on residual over-collected data that resides in the firm also become more secure as a new source of value if it can be used within the firm.

Data markets provide a way of capturing value, but so too do digital platforms accumulating a resource accreting inside them due to its increasing property rights security as the affiliated specific purpose data is targeted for political bargaining and clarification of property rights and obligations, sharpening the value of the residual. The process by which stronger property rights are created is by the legislative and regulatory process of making clear what they are. The firm then owns everything that is 'not that', that is, the negative image of that which has been clarified. The key idea is that the discovery of property rights and data rights on behalf of consumers strengthens the residual by making it tested against a claim. Of course, that residual data is trapped. It has to be used in situ. But this predicts that specialised technology platforms will eventually evolve into data companies as the data rights vest in the firm. The value of the property rights will be extracted in the equity value of the firm. The rise in the value of data as inputs into economic production, coupled with the explosion of technologies for generating and uploading data, means that it is economically worth creating property rights. Data has value only at scale and so platforms have an incentive to get very big in order to exploit this effect.

6 Adaptation and Agency in the Supertransition

Successfully navigating the supertransition (i.e. propelling us towards a more open, decentralised and global economy) requires adaptation under extreme uncertainty. This uncertainty is not purely technological, such as wondering what AI capabilities will be released open-source and go viral on social media tomorrow. We must also adapt to a cloud of uncertainty as we shift to digital institutions. In this section we examine the supertransition through the eyes of entrepreneurs, established organisations, policymakers, and workers. Throughout, we emphasise the need for adaptive strategies under institutional uncertainty – whether it be entrepreneurs building one-person unicorns, established organisations becoming more open, policymakers grappling with permissionless innovation, or workers becoming more agentic. The supertransition will be a bumpy ride.

6.1 Entrepreneurship

Innovation propels economic evolution, and entrepreneurs both drive and must adapt to institutional acceleration. As Joseph Schumpeter (1942) described, the 'gale of creative destruction' continually makes existing products, services, and business models obsolete. But institutional acceleration does more than speed up this gale – it fundamentally changes how entrepreneurs must operate in an open, complex, and global context. It is well understood that entrepreneurs must grapple with institutional uncertainty (Bylund and McCaffrey 2017). Technological combinatorics represents not just new products and services, but an acceleration of reorganisation in our institutional systems, generating deeper uncertainty for entrepreneurs.

The supertransition shifts the optimal organisational structure of entrepreneurial ventures. The transformation is driven by a radical reduction in costs associated with launching new ventures. Rather than hiring teams of specialists, the minimum viable resources needed to launch a new venture are more open, composable, and accessible to the lone entrepreneur. As co-founder of OpenAI Sam Altman claims, soon we will see the first one-person unicorn (billion-dollar valuation) company.

The techno-vectors we described earlier lower the costs of spinning up new entrepreneurial ventures. These advanced tools allow entrepreneurs to bundle and compose complex technological solutions with minimal technical expertise. For instance, AI-powered agents can handle tasks ranging from customer service to complex data analysis. These technologies have increasingly toolkit-like features – meaning that entrepreneurs can bundle and compose them together while understanding fewer of the underlying technological aspects.

This technological empowerment of individual entrepreneurs challenges traditional notions of firm structure and organisation. Foss and Klein (2012) argue that the organisational structure an entrepreneur creates – the *firm* – is an integral part of the entrepreneurial process itself. They posit that the firm is not merely a formal contractual arrangement, but is a manifestation of the entrepreneur's judgement about how to optimally combine resources. Because of the lower costs of producing within the boundaries of a firm, the organisational structure through the supertransition will be smaller and more deeply embedded with automated tooling. Some successful entrepreneurs will be able to navigate this new approach to entrepreneurship that doesn't quickly, or even at all, move to scaling a team of human assets. Entrepreneurs will need 'combinatorial alertness' to how multiple frontier technologies can combine to create entirely new markets and transform institutional structures.

The modern economy emerged through increasing specialisation and trade. Indeed, the businesses that entrepreneurs build in the supertransition will become increasingly specialised, occupying particular institutional niches enabled by combinatorics. But for entrepreneurs to realise the value of these niches they will, perhaps ironically, need to be more generalist. There will be a premium for generalist skills (at least in the short term) where entrepreneurs can be combinatorially alert across previously unconnected domains.

Technological combinatorics expands the design space of entrepreneurial opportunities. This is not to say that there are no returns from specialisation, but that the space that combinatorics opens up will reveal value in the capacity for generalist entrepreneurs to combine techno-vectors. The rise of generative AI is a useful tool for entrepreneurs only to automate some of their tasks at low cost, but to rapidly learn and pivot as they adapt.

Institutional acceleration is not all good news for the entrepreneur. In a world of more open, permissionless, and composable technological tools, the traditional technology 'moat' will be harder to find, let alone sustain. Open tools propel combinatorics, but they also prevent lock-in of business models and networks. While it is becoming easier and cheaper to combine new technologies into feasible businesses, those tools are available to everyone. Unprecedented levels of company launches – including one person unicorns – are not far away. Yet while there may be more businesses, servicing a more complex economic structure, we can also expect the average success and life of a business to decline.

6.2 Evolving Established Organisations

The supertransition will be driven not only by start-ups combining new techno-vectors, but also by established organisations adapting to a radically new competitive environment. How should these organisations navigate this transformation?

Institutional combinatorics means that many of the organisations that survive the supertransition will be unrecognisable. They will be unbundled, reorganised and will pivot to new parts of the economic system. This raises hard questions. How do managers incentivise technological combinatorics? What does institutional acceleration mean for hierarchies? Will established organisations simply be outcompeted by smaller entrepreneurial start-ups who are less-encumbered by entrenched structures?

Managers should have two key objectives in mind. First, institutional acceleration creates more knowledge and enables us to compute that knowledge into value. New technological combinations propel institutional acceleration, which ultimately enables us to use more and better knowledge to coordinate. Second, as Friedrich A. Hayek noted, competition is a 'procedure for discovering facts which, if the procedure did not exist, would remain unknown or at least would not be used' (Hayek 2002). Established organisations must drive experimentation across their organisation at different levels to discover this knowledge.

6.2.1 Shadow Combinatorial Innovation

It would be easy for managers of established firms to think that institutional acceleration will be driven by them. This is how industrial innovation has been imagined for a century. But the low-cost nature of the techno-vectors we have described earlier suggests that this experimentation will be increasingly driven by employees, from the bottom-up. For instance, employees using generative AI tools without management oversight. We call this 'shadow combinatorial innovation' (Waters-Lynch et al. 2024). Today's employees are the entrepreneurial drivers who are discovering and implementing valuable technological combinations within existing organisational structures, often without formal oversight. They stay in the shadows for many, including fears about job security, or simply to maintain a competitive edge with less effort. The result is that potentially valuable innovations are not translated into company-wide capabilities. They may also not benefit from entrepreneurial activity that happens in teams rather than individually (see Harper 2008).

A common management response to shadow combinatorial innovation might be to prevent it. To push more security features onto company-owned hardware. To punish unauthorised use of new technologies in the workplace. But ultimately shadow combinatorial innovation benefits firms – employees, with their localised knowledge of tasks and challenges, are well placed to find new efficiencies. While managers might think that can drive institutional acceleration from above, they often lack the specific knowledge to identify the most valuable technological combinations. Remember: institutional acceleration is a discovery process.

Rather than simply being permissive of shadow combinatorial innovation, organisations may need to actively harness it. Managers might seek to develop incentives for employees not only to innovate, but also to reveal that information to others. One approach is to foster 'communities of practice' or 'innovation commons', where employees can share knowledge about opportunities without fear, fostering open innovation that aligns individual and organisational goals. For instance, a firm might implement an internal platform for anonymous sharing of AI-driven innovations, with rewards for beneficial contributions.

6.2.2 Composable Organisations

If established firms want to survive the supertransition, they will need to transition from closed hierarchical organisations to more composable and open organisations. In the previous section we described how that can happen internally, through incentivising combinatorial innovation within the firm. But this also needs to happen across organisational boundaries. Combinatorial innovation means composable organisations are comparatively effective institutional forms, enabling firms to specialise in their core competencies while coordinating with others to deliver complex products or services.

New technologies have long lowered the costs of creating more composable organisations. For instance, firms can use blockchain-based trust to become more modular and specialised, conducting some coordination across digital infrastructure rather than integrating them into the firm (Berg et al. 2019). Not only does combinatorial innovation enable new types of composable organisations, but the environment of institutional acceleration creates new competitive pressures for organisations to become more composable. Organisations that fail to create mechanisms for coordinating and combining with external partners and technologies will be outcompeted. Only by combining and recombining in a composable way will they discover how to drive more compute into their organisation.

6.3 Policy and Institutional Acceleration

6.3.1 The Problem of Pacing Institutional Acceleration

Policymakers respond slowly to frontier technologies, creating a growing gap between technological change and regulatory systems' ability to keep up – the 'pacing problem' (Marchant 2020). This gap acts as a drag on technological change and institutional acceleration, driven by fundamental uncertainty about technological impacts. As Collingridge (1982) writes, when technologies are easiest to control in their early stages, regulators lack the knowledge to do so effectively.

The supertransition exacerbates the pacing problem in two main ways. First, the combinatorics of frontier technologies creates *acceleration*. The gap between regulatory frameworks and technological innovation widens as regulators struggle with limited resources. While regulators grapple with individual technologies like cryptocurrencies and AI in isolation, these technologies are already combining into more complex forms like autonomous agents using blockchain-based smart contracts. Second, this acceleration is fundamentally *institutional*. The technologies we've described have deep institutional effects when combined. Regulators, experienced with industrial and centralised technologies, now face radical new institutional forms. Policymakers are still grappling with regulating centralised digital platforms that have jurisdictional homes, let alone decentralised digital platforms that are borderless and community owned.

Predicting and responding to one technology is hard, let alone responding to a combinatorial explosion. To make good policy, regulators need to have an idea what a technology is for, and, throughout the supertransition, how those technologies might be combined in an increasing institutional design space. But that information is only revealed through a competitive market process – the process of combinatorics itself.

6.3.2 Anti-Trajectory Innovation Policy

Innovation policy in the twentieth century was largely built around individual technological trajectories, viewing advancement as following predictable paths. Everett Rogers described how innovations typically diffuse through society following an S-shaped curve: slow initial adoption by innovators, followed by rapid diffusion as the technology gains mainstream acceptance, and finally reaching a plateau as the market saturates (Rogers et al. 2014). This trajectory thinking has profoundly influenced modern innovation policy, both explicitly and implicitly (Dosi 1982), through targeted incentives and mission-oriented programs like DARPA in the United States or the European Union's Horizon Europe initiative (McCloskey and Mingardi 2020, Mazzucato 2021).

However, trajectory thinking emerged in an era of industrial technologies with limited composability – manufacturing techniques in automobiles had little influence on pharmaceuticals or telecommunications. While individual trajectories exist today, they are insufficient in an environment of institutional combinatorics. The technologies driving the supertransition are highly composable and interact across domains in complex ways. This limitation of trajectory thinking mirrors the difference between partial and general equilibrium analysis in economics – where partial equilibrium focuses on a single market in isolation, general equilibrium considers the interactions between all markets simultaneously. Similarly, trajectory thinking fails to capture the full complexity of interactions between various technological and institutional innovations in the digital economy.

Persisting with trajectory-based approaches in policymaking could actively distort the combinatorial nature of innovation in the supertransition. Rather than supporting individual trajectories, innovation policy must focus on enabling combinatorial innovation through institutional experimentation and exit options.

6.3.3 Institutional Exit

Governments have traditionally responded to regulatory challenges through permissioned exit mechanisms like 'regulatory sandboxes', 'special jurisdictions', and 'special economic zones'. Each of these is a mechanism of exit – they allow controlled experimentation with new business models or access to alternative institutional environments. A regulatory sandbox enables exit to a supervised environment to try new business models; a special jurisdiction enables businesses and individuals to access an alternative institutional environment (such as courts) in an adjacent physical jurisdiction. Such permissioned exit can help regulators discover knowledge and place competitive forces on host institutions. But institutional acceleration describes a process whereby private actors and communities are combining frontier technologies to create new institutions.

Institutional acceleration comes through the rapid and pervasive discovery of new types of digital institutions that are enabled by technological combinations. The technological combinatorics that happens throughout the supertransition gives us new ways to solve problems that might have previously been solved through other institutional coordination mechanisms. While frontier technologies can cause harms, dampening institutional acceleration would be too costly.

Thierer (2016) distinguishes his permissionless innovation approach from the precautionary principle – where in making decisions about new technologies regulators err on the side of protecting against hypothetical harms, rather than enabling a technology to develop to realise the future benefits. Thierer suggests that regulators should shift attention from regulating ex ante innovation, to regulating harms that arise from innovations ex post. This process reveals information about new technologies through the competitive market process, rather than suppressing them before we even try.

But the supertransition needs a more extreme stance of permissionless innovation – one that recognises that we are exiting and building new types of private digital institutions. The challenge that regulators face isn't one or a few industrial technologies that, after we have applied them in the wild, we will reveal some harms, and then we can remedy those harms in court. We need permissionless innovation because the supertransition is itself the build-out of new digital institutions. If institutional acceleration is left to take its course, then the result won't simply be ex post remedies in court, but a replacement of many of the basic functions of our institutional order. In the calculus of the costs of suppressing or enabling a new technology, the costs of suppressing a technology in the supertransition are much higher.

6.3.4 Experimental Policy

Policy is a discovery process. Just as entrepreneurs combine technologies to create new institutional forms, policymakers must experiment with regulatory approaches to find effective governance models for the digital economy. To facilitate this discovery process, governments should optimise for discovery and learning, rather than control. Some of this experimentation should happen in the government itself. Ultimately the government is an institution, and it will also need to institutionally evolve. Some of these experiments will be counter-intuitive, such as randomised trials of 'experimental elimination' (Potts 2010).

There are other areas of more unexpected policy that will shape the speed and success of the supertransition. For instance, free speech provides a foundation for innovation. Freedom of speech is a fundamental liberty and a necessary precondition for the open society – a society open to new ideas, experimentation, and the free exchange of knowledge. In an open society, individuals are free to challenge prevailing norms, propose new concepts, and engage in open debate. John Stuart Mill (1859) argued that the freedom to express and debate ideas, even incorrect ideas, is essential for the advancement of knowledge.

Freedom of speech is a driver of combinatorial innovation, enabling the free flow of information and ideas essential for combining different technologies in novel ways. Digital platforms like GitHub facilitate this through open-source practices, allowing developers to share innovations, learn from each other, and build upon each other's work. This combination and recombination of technologies are key drivers of innovation. Similarly, platforms like arXiv and SSRN allow for the open sharing of academic research, which accelerates the dissemination of new ideas and fosters collaboration. When individuals are free to express themselves without fear of censorship, they are more likely to share their knowledge and collaborate with others. This open exchange of information creates an environment where ideas can cross-pollinate and combine.

In this sense, the unique protection of freedom of expression by the US First Amendment is a global subsidy for innovation. Regardless of where they are domiciled, individuals and firms can distribute information through US-hosted platforms like GitHub and arXiv and benefit from a jurisprudence that has established – at least in the lower courts – that computer code is the equivalent of speech and deserves the same protections as (for example) political speech.

6.3.5 A Recalibrated State

One impact of the pressures of institutional acceleration may be a recalibration of the state. States may become smaller, focusing on core functions and embracing principles-based regulation that can withstand rapid change. This change will not be by choice, but through competitive pressures from more open, decentralised, and global digital institutions.

This recalibration is driven by the accelerating pace of institutional change and the increasingly porous boundaries between digital entities and objects. Applying conventional regulatory frameworks, designed for clearly delineated industries and institutional archetypes, will become increasingly challenging. Short-term effective regulatory approaches will therefore emphasise adaptation and openness, including within the state itself.

But the dynamics of institutional acceleration will continue to push many digital institutions beyond the reach of conventional state control. Operating across jurisdictions on decentralised rails, these new digital institutions and infrastructure will highlight the shortcomings of existing regulations. The cryptoeconomy already highlights these regulatory challenges, and technological combinatorics (such as blockchain-based DAOs as AI governance) will only intensify them.

In response, we anticipate a strategic retreat of the state to core functions and principles-based regulation. The future state will focus on maintaining fundamental societal guardrails while allowing digital institutions to be built and compete with it. States will need to rediscover their core comparative advantage as an institutional system.

6.4 Agency and the Supertransition

We have analysed the supertransition through the lens of the entrepreneur, business leader, and policymaker. But maybe you don't fit into these categories. Perhaps you're an employee, a citizen or a volunteer. What, then? In many ways you still face a fundamental challenge of the supertransition: acting more 'agentically' – that is, taking control.

Being agentic means actively engaging with new digital tools, even frontier tools and institutions that don't quite work yet. It means choosing which institutions to use, and when to use them, rather than adopting the default institutional set. It means building adapting strategies into your own life workflow. These approaches are intimately familiar to entrepreneurs, who must adopt these strategies. But they are less common in the relatively stable pre-supertransition economy.

Becoming more agentic isn't just about acting within existing rule systems or choosing between them. It means shifting towards building and shaping institutions themselves. We will all become more entrepreneurial, knitting together tools and technologies into new businesses and workflows. For many people it won't be enough merely to adapt to new institutions. Institutional accelerationism, as we will introduce it in the final section, means we must advocate for them – that is, actively participating in their development.

7 i/acc

Some 250 years ago, the agrarian-feudal economy of Western Europe began to transform into an industrial economy. What caused the 'industrial revolution'? Technological innovations in steam, steel, textiles, railways and so on is the standard explanation. Yet the deeper reason was the prior 'institutional revolution' in property rights that created the incentive structure for industrial production and investment to flourish (Allen 2011). Our thesis in this Element has been that we are today in the early phases of a new transformation from an industrial economy to a digital economy. The proximate cause of this 'digital revolution' is another cluster of advanced technologies – computers, internet, cloud, IoT, robots, blockchains, AI, and so on, powering economic growth. But we see a deeper transformation at work too – the digital economy is also a profound institutional revolution.

The essential definition of a digital economy is not digital production and consumption (although plainly includes this), it is digital institutions. When property rights, incentive mechanisms, and rules that create economic order are all fundamentally digital, then we have a digital economy. The conditions for this have been mostly laid during the past 60–80 years, and the arrival of the cluster of 'new institutional technologies' is the beginning of a new age of digital economies with institutions that are advanced by computational engines that can be innovated on.

An economy is a device, made of institutional rules and their enforcement, to solve the problem of cooperation between strangers to mutually create and distribute value with whatever resources are available. To do so at scale, institutions must powerfully align individual incentives with socially desirable actions. These rules must work efficiently. They must lower transaction costs and connect to all the factors of production including resources, capital, and knowledge. They must also minimise anything left out (i.e. *externalities*). For these rules to work well, and to also be easily upgraded and to experience innovation, they benefit from being natively digital.

This process is what we have described as the supertransition. The superstransition is powering institutional acceleration. And institutional acceleration is one of the most important factors in the world today in understanding economic dynamics. So, what is the ideology of institutional accelerationism? If I am an institutional accelerationist, as we hope you are now, what do I believe?

A few years ago we wrote a book about the economic significance of blockchain, calling it 'institutional cryptoeconomics'. We took the domain of 'cryptoeconomics' – which is economic theory (information economics and mechanism design, an application of game theory) applied to design of blockchain-based economic systems – and instead pushed it through the analytic framework of institutional economics. Our insight was that blockchains (i.e. distributed ledgers, tokens, smart contracts, consensus mechanism) provided a new technical foundation for institutions, and could be the base layer for a new digital economy. This same insight has been developed by others too, for instance, in Balaji Srinivasan's *Network State,* or in Primavera de Filippi and Jessie-Kate Schingler's concept of *Network Nations*, both exploring how blockchain technologies can enable exit to new self-sovereign communities.

Now extend this vision of distributed compute technologies to the other digital technologies that wrap digital compute in things (IoT, GenAI). Then add a global network of low latency and fast compute through cheap ubiquitous relays (cloud and LEO database, cubesats, oracles). Then accelerate that compute speed and depth (quantum). Then overlay with ubiquitous human natural language interface and expertise (GenAI again). Then make it informationally safe (cyber). Now we are converging on the foundational infrastructure for a new type of private order economy. During the first wave of computing and the internet, the revolutionary technological affordances of ICT were information processing and communication (e.g. signal processing, computers, databases, telecommunications, networking hardware). But now, the revolutionary technological affordances are a different species of ICT: an institutional coordination technology.

Prior to 1776, in the opening pages of *The Wealth of Nations*, Adam Smith looked out upon the semi-feudal agricultural lands south of Glasgow and saw an anachronism, an object out of time. The industrial revolution and the market capitalist economies that he described in that now-celebrated pin factory were decades in the future. The frontier technologies we describe here are also institutional anachronisms. Instead, we suggest understanding this Element as a work of 'Hayekian techno-futurism'. But what we seek to describe is a new economic order made of abstract rules running on distributed digital technologies. It is Hayekian because this is about the use of knowledge in society. It is techno-futurist because we are trying to understand the future.

Compare the different consequences of speed of change. Fast technological change is better than slow because of accumulated benefits. Where technological improvement allows greater outputs for constant inputs the productivity gain can be spent in various ways.[10] In a Malthusian model (Galor 2011, 2022), technological improvement is spent on population growth, so aggregate utility increases. In modern growth models, productivity increases consumption, so individual utility increases. But rapid institutional change is not always beneficial. Edmund Burke (1790), for instance, argued that political revolutions, which overthrow established orders, can lead to instability and unintended consequences. The philosophy of liberal conservatism, for instance, can be for industrial technological change and against institutional change. The reasons for this are due to the evolved character of many institutions, and so the reasons why they work may be difficult to formulate (Hayek 1960), but also an institutional order requires persistence and predictability to facilitate long-range coordination in space and time (Kydland and Prescott 1982). Institutional technologies tend to be deep rules that are very costly to make and change (Williamson 2000). They are often embodied or hard-coded in nation states in the culture of the people, in the organisation of its capital, and in its laws and legislation.

The philosophy of *i/acc* has another intellectual origin, namely in e/acc, or effective accelerationism, which is a recent philosophy movement that is explicitly pro-technology and hardcore techno-optimist. Each of us has followed closely, and sometimes participated in, the e/acc themed debates that have arisen to prominence in the wake of the release of OpenAI's ChatGPT models around AI 'safety'. More broadly, we have a long track record of fighting the many enemies of new technology and innovation. We are unashamedly and thoroughly on the public record as being against safetyism and the precautionary principle in public policy, and extremely pro-free speech and open innovation (e.g. see Berg 2012, 2018, Allen et al. 2020, Potts 2019). We were early campaigners for freedom for autonomous drone technology. We have spent the last seven years making the case for blockchain technology as

---

[10] Known as Hicks-neutral or homothetic technological change.

a viable way for voluntary communities to rebuild the foundational infrastructure for new economies at global scale.

In *The New Technologies of Freedom* we laid out an optimistic case for institutional change through technology. Rather than achieving institutional change through the slow, grinding, and ineffective paths of politics, we argued that people should build new institutions (Allen et al. 2020). That vision and mechanism of institutional evolution is only possible in a world of open, composable, and low-cost tools for building new institutions. But once we have them, as we now do, we can build new institutions – property rights, contracts, organisations, identities – that embed the types of values and rights we want into digital rules. Rather than seeking consensus over some jurisdictionally determined arbitrary boundary, we can create new institutional niches, and sort ourselves amongst them. The philosophy of *i/acc* embodies this optimistic approach to institutional evolution.

The core of *e/acc* is being optimistic about the trajectory of tech acceleration, and that the answer to any problems met along the way is more technology (e.g. Deutsch 2011). It is also a way of painting the barriers to technological progress as things to be overcome, such as safetyist regulation or precautionary policy agendas.

But our *i/acc* argument here has been that the system itself is evolving, and should continue to evolve, a new defence mechanism in the form of what we style as institutional acceleration. As digital technologies unfold and develop the space of economic institutions, they become their own environment (what evolutionary biologists call a niche), setting up a new form of dynamic process that works through its own evolutionary logic. The benefits of applying technology extend beyond just more economic freedoms, choice, and prosperity. Indeed, technologies can help solve sustainability challenges by enabling better coordination around environmental resources through property rights definition, monitoring, and exchange. And that there are feedback loops from this.

Our view, then, is that technologies are evolving, which is causing institutions to evolve, which is causing economies to evolve. This is an autocatalytic process, because that economic evolution is in turn driving further technological evolution. This Element has sought to describe the way that this process is unfolding, and what we might do about it, through a particular juncture we have called the supertransition.

References

'Google: "We have no moat, and neither does OpenAI"' (2023). *Semianalysis*, May 4.

Acemoglu, D. and Robinson, J.A. (2012). *Why Nations Fail: The Origins of Power, Prosperity, and Poverty*. New York: Crown.

Agar, J. (2003). *The Government Machine: A Revolutionary History of the Computer, History of Computing*. Cambridge, MA: MIT Press.

Agrawal, A., Gans, J., and Goldfarb, A. (2018). *Prediction Machines: The Simple Economics of Artificial Intelligence*. Boston: Harvard Business Review Press.

Agrawal, A., Gans, J., and Goldfarb, A. (2022). *Power and Prediction: The Disruptive Economics of Artificial Intelligence*. Boston: Harvard Business Review Press.

Agrawal, A., McHale, J., and Oettl, A. (2018). Finding needles in haystacks: Artificial intelligence and recombinant growth. In A. Agrawal, J. Gans, and A. Goldfarb (eds.), *The Economics of Artificial Intelligence*, pp. 149–174. Chicago: University of Chicago Press.

Allen, D. (2011). *The Institutional Revolution*. Chicago: University of Chicago Press.

Allen, D. W. E., Berg, C., and Davidson, S. (2020). *The New Technologies of Freedom*. Great Barrington, MA: American Institute for Economic Research.

Allen, D. W. E., Berg, C., Lane, A. M., MacDonald, T., and Potts, J. (2023). The exchange theory of web3 governance. *Kyklos*, 76(4), 659–675.

Allen, D. W. E., Berg, C., Markey-Towler, B., Novak, M., and Potts, J. (2020). Blockchain and the evolution of institutional technologies: Implications for innovation policy. *Research Policy*, 49(1), 103865.

Allen, D. W. E. and Lane, A. M. (2024). Smart Contracts as Private Governance Tools. *SSRN 4598625*.

Allen, D. W. E. and Potts, J. (2016). How innovation commons contribute to discovering and developing new technologies. *International Journal of the Commons*, 10(2), 1035–1054.

Allen, D. W. E. and Potts, J. (2023). Web3 toolkits: A user innovation theory of crypto development. *Journal of Open Innovation: Technology, Market, and Complexity*, 9(2), 100050.

Almudi, I. and Fatas-Villafranca, F. (2021). *Coevolution in Economic Systems: Cambridge Elements in Evolutionary Economics*. Cambridge: Cambridge University Press.

Alston, E., Law, W., Murtazashvili, I., and Weiss, M. (2022). Blockchain networks as constitutional and competitive polycentric orders. *Journal of Institutional Economics*, 18(5), 707–723.

Ambury, J. and German, A. (eds.) (2019). *Knowledge and Ignorance of Self in Platonic Philosophy*. New York: Cambridge University Press.

Aoki, M. (2007). Endogenizing institutions and institutional changes. *Journal of Institutional Economics*, 3(1), 1–31.

Arnold, D., Saniie, J., and Heifetz, A. (2022). Homomorphic encryption for machine learning and artificial intelligence applications. Argonne National Lab, Argonne, IL.

Arrow, K. (1962). Economic welfare and allocation of resources for invention. In R. Nelson (ed.), *The Rate and Direction of Inventive Activity: Economic and Social Factors*, pp. 609–626. Princeton: Princeton University Press.

Arthur, W. B. (2009). *The Nature of Technology*. New York: Free Press.

Babbage, C. (2010). *Babbage's Calculating Engines: Being a Collection of Papers Relating to Them; Their History and Construction*. Edited by H. P. Babbage. Cambridge: Cambridge University Press.

Bailey, A. M., Rettler, B., & Warmke, C. (2024). *Resistance Money: A Philosophical Case for Bitcoin*. Taylor & Francis: Abingdon, Oxfordshire, United Kingdom.

Bao, Z., Luo, M., Wang, H., Choo, K. K. R., & He, D. (2021). Blockchain-based secure communication for space information networks. *IEEE Network*, 35(4), 50–57.

Baran, P. (1964). On distributed communications networks. *IEEE transactions on Communications Systems*, 12(1), 1–9.

Baruch, M., Drucker, N., Greenberg, L., & Moshkowich, G. (2022). A methodology for training homomorphic encryption friendly neural networks. In J. Zhou, Adepu, S., Alcaraz, C., et al. (eds.), *Applied Cryptography and Network Security Workshops*, pp. 536–553. Cham: Springer.

Basalla, G. (1988). *The evolution of technology*. Cambridge: Cambridge University Press.

Batty, M. (2013). *The New Science of Cities*. Cambridge, MA: MIT Press.

Ben-Aaron, D. (1985). Weizenbaum examines computers and society. *The Tech*, 105(16).

Berg, C. (2012). *In Defence of Freedom of Speech*. Institute of Public Affairs and Mannkal Economic Education Foundation: Perth, Australia.

Berg, C. (2018). *The Classical Liberal Case for Privacy in a World of Surveillance and Technological Change*. Cham: Palgrave Macmillan.

Berg, C., Davidson, S., and Potts, J. (2018). Beyond money: Cryptocurrencies, machine mediated transactions, and high-frequency hyperbarter. *SSRN*.

Berg, C., Davidson, S., and Potts, J. (2019). *Understanding the Blockchain Economy*. Cheltenham: Edward Elgar.

Berg, C., Davidson, S., and Potts, J. (2023). Institutions to constrain chaotic robots: Why generative AI needs blockchain. *SSRN*.

Berg, C. and Potts, J. (2024). The institutional economics of quantum computing. *Medium*, 19 June.

Bennett, C. H. and Brassard, G. (2014). Quantum cryptography: Public key distribution and coin tossing. *Theoretical Computer Science*, 560, 7–11.

Besley, T. and Persson T. (2009). The origins of state capacity: Property rights, taxation, and politics. *American Economic Review*, 99(4), 1218–1244.

Bettencourt, L. (2013). The origins of scaling in cities. *Science*, 340, 1438–1441.

Bhatia, M. and Sood, S. (2020). Quantum computing-inspired network optimization for IoT applications. *IEEE Internet of Things Journal*, 7(6), 5590–5598.

Bloom, N., Van Reenen, J., and Williams, H. (2019). A toolkit of policies to promote innovation. *Journal of Economic Perspectives*, 33(3), 163–184.

Bova, F., Goldfarb, A., and Melko, R. (2021). Commercial applications of quantum computing. *EPJ Quantum Technology*, 8(1), 1–13.

Bremner, M., Devitt, S., and Zerenturk, E. (2024). Quantum algorithms and applications. Office of the NSW Chief Scientist & Engineer, March.

Broadbent, A., Kazmi, R. A., and Minwalla, C. (2024). A quantum vault scheme for digital currency. *arXiv*.

Brynjolfsson, E., Li, D., and Raymond, L. (2023). Generative AI at work. *Working Paper Series, National Bureau of Economic Research*.

Brynjolfsson, E., Rock, D., & Syverson, C. (2021). The productivity J-curve: How intangibles complement general purpose technologies. *American Economic Journal: Macroeconomics*, 13(1), 333–372.

Buchanan, J. and Tullock, G. (1962). *The Calculus of Consent*. Ann Arbor: University of Michigan Press.

Burke, E. (1790). *Reflections of the Revolution in France*. London: J. Dodsley.

Buterin, V., Hitzig, Z., and Weyl, E. G. (2019). A flexible design for funding public goods. *Management Science*, 65(11), 5171–5187.

Bylund, P. L. & McCaffrey, M. (2017). A theory of entrepreneurship and institutional uncertainty. *Journal of Business Venturing*, 32(5), 461–475.

Cacciapuoti, A. S., Caleffi, M., Tafuri, F., Cataliotti, F. S., Gherardini, S., & Bianchi, G. (2019). Quantum internet: Networking challenges in distributed quantum computing. *IEEE Network*, 34(1), 137–143.

Coladangelo, A. and Sattath, O. (2020). A quantum money solution to the blockchain scalability problem. *Quantum*, 4, 1–44.

Collingridge, D. (1982). *The Social Control of Technology*. New York: St Martin's Press.

Corbett, J. C., Dean, J., Epstein, M., et al. (2013). Spanner: Google's globally distributed database. *ACM Transactions on Computer Systems*, 31(3), 1–22.

Cortada, J. (2011). *Information and the Modern Corporation*. Cambridge, MA: MIT Press.

Coyle, D., Kay, L., Diepeveen, S., Tennison, J., & Wdowin, J. (2020). *The Value of Data: Policy Implications*. Bennett Institute for Public Policy, University of Cambridge; Open Data Institute.

Cui, Z., Demirer, M., Jaffe, S., et al. (2024). The effects of generative AI on high skilled work: Evidence from three field experiments with software developers. *SSRN Scholarly Paper*, Rochester.

Davidson, S., De Filippi, P., and Potts, J. (2018). Blockchains and the economic institutions of capitalism. *Journal of Institutional Economics*, 14(4), 639–658.

Davidson, S., Mohan, V., and Potts, J. (2020). Location, taxation and governments: An exchange theory of intellectual property. *Journal of Economic Behavior & Organization*, 169, 266–283.

Davies, A. (2004). Computational intermediation and the evolution of computation as a commodity. *Applied Economics*, 36(11), 1131–1142.

De Filippi, P., Reijers, W., and Mannan, M. (2024). *Blockchain Governance*. Cambridge, MA: MIT Press.

De Filippi, P. and Wright, A. (2018). *Blockchain and the Law: The Rule of Code*. Cambridge, MA: Harvard University Press.

de Forges de Parny, L., Alibart, O., Debaud, J. et al. (2023). Satellite-based quantum information networks: Use cases, architecture, and roadmap. *Communications Physics*, 6(1), 1–17.

Deloitte Space (2022). The commercialization of low earth orbit, Vol. 2. www2.deloitte.com/content/dam/Deloitte/us/Documents/public-sector/us-gps-the-commercialization-of-leo-vol-2-an-orbit-for-everyone.pdf.

Deutsch, D. (1985). Quantum theory, the Church–Turing principle and the universal quantum computer. *Proceedings of the Royal Society of London. A. Mathematical and Physical Sciences*, 400(1818), 97–117,

Deutsch, D. (1997). Quantum theory, the church – Turing principle and the universal quantum computer. *Proceedings of the Royal Society of London A: Mathematical and Physical Sciences*, 400(1818), 97–117.

Deutsch, D. (2011). *The Beginning of Infinity*. London: Penguin.

Dieks, D. (1982). Communication by EPR devices. *Physics Letters A*, 92(6), 271–272.

Diffie, W., & Hellman, M. E. (1976, June). *Multiuser cryptographic techniques*. In *Proceedings of the June 7-10, 1976, National Computer Conference and Exposition* (pp. 109–112). New York: ACM.

Dopfer, K., & Potts, J. (2007). *The general theory of economic evolution*. London: Routledge.

Dosi, G. (1982). Technological paradigms and technological trajectories: A suggested interpretation of the determinants and directions of technical change. *Research Policy*, 11(3), 147–162.

Douceur, J. R. (2002). The Sybil attack. In P. Druschel, F. Kaashoek, A. Rowstron (eds.), *International Workshop on Peer-to-Peer Systems*, pp. 251–260. Cambridge, MA: Springer.

Eichengreen, B. (2015). Secular stagnation: The long view. *American Economic Review*, 105(5), 66–70.

Feynman, R. (1982). Simulating physics with computers. *International Journal of Theoretical Physics*, 21(6), 467–488.

Feynman, R. (1986). Quantum mechanical computers. *Foundations of Physics*, 16(6), 507–531.

Fitzsimons, J. F. (2017). Private quantum computation: An introduction to blind quantum computing and related protocols. *NPJ Quantum Information*, 3(23), 1–11.

Foss, N. and Klein, P. (2012). *Organizing Entrepreneurial Judgment: A New Approach to the Firm*. Cambridge: Cambridge University Press.

Freeman, C. and Soete, L. (1997). *Economics of Industrial Innovation*, 3rd ed. Cambridge, MA: MIT Press.

Frolov, D. (2021). Blockchain and institutional complexity: An extended institutional approach. *Journal of Institutional Economics*, 17(1), 21–36.

Galor, O. (2011). *Unified Growth Theory*. Princeton: Princeton University Press.

Galor, O. (2022). *The Journey of Humanity and the Keys to Human Progress*. New York: Penguin.

Gatti, R., Koppl, R., Fath, B., et al. (2020). On the emergence of ecological and economic niches. *Journal of Bioeconomics*, 22(1), 99–127.

Giovannetti, V., Lloyd, S., and Maccone, L. (2008). Quantum private queries. *Physical Review Letters*, 100(23), 230502.

Glaeser, E., La Porta, R., Lopez-de-Silanes, F., and Shleifer, A. (2004). Do institutions cause growth? *Journal of Economic Growth*, 9(3), 271–303.

Goldfarb, A. and Tucker, C. (2019). Digital economics. *Journal Economic Literature*, 57(1), 3–43.

Gordon, R. (2018). Why has economic growth slowed when innovation appears to be accelerating? *National Bureau of Economic Research Working Paper No. w24554*.

Graeber, D. and Wengrow, D. (2021). *The Dawn of Everything*. London: Penguin UK.

Greenstein, S. (2017). *How the Internet Became Commercial*. Princeton: Princeton University Press.

Grover, L. K. (1996). A fast quantum mechanical algorithm for database search. In G. L. Miller (ed.), *Proceedings of the Twenty-Eighth Annual ACM Symposium on Theory of Computing*, pp. 212–219. New York: Association for Computing Machinery.

Gujju, Y., Matsuo, A., and Raymond, R. (2024). Quantum machine learning on near-term quantum devices: Current state of supervised and unsupervised techniques for real-world applications. *Physical Review Applied*, 21(6), 067001.

Haring, K. (2007). *Ham Radio's Technical Culture*. Cambridge, MA: MIT Press.

Harper, D. (2008). Towards a theory of entrepreneurial teams. *Journal of Business Venturing*, 23(6), 613–626.

Harper, D. (2013). Property rights, entrepreneurship and coordination. *Journal of Economic Behavior and Organization*, 88(1), 62–77.

Harwick, C. and Caton, J. (2022). What's holding back blockchain finance? On the possibility of decentralized autonomous finance. *Quarterly Review of Economics and Finance*, 84, 420–429.

Hayek, F. A. (1945). Use of knowledge in society. *American Economic Review*, 35(4), 519–530.

Hayek, F. A. (1960). *The Constitution of Liberty*. Chicago: University of Chicago Press.

Hayek, F. A. (1973). *Law, Legislation, and Liberty* (3 vols.). Chicago: University of Chicago Press.

Hayek, F. A. (2002). Competition as a discovery procedure. *Quarterly Journal of Austrian Economics*, 5(3), 9–23.

Heiner, R. (1983). The origin of predictable behavior. *American Economic Review*, 73(4), 560–595.

Hellman, M. and Yost, J. (2014). An interview with Martin Hellman. 22 November.

Henrich, J. (2020). *The WEIRDest People in the World: How the West Became Psychologically Peculiar and Particularly Prosperous*. New York: Farrar, Straus and Giroux.

Hidalgo, C. (2015). *Why Information Grows: The Evolution of Order, from Atoms to Economies*. New York: Basic Books.

Highfill, T. and Weinzierl, M. (2024). Real growth in space manufacturing output substantially exceeds growth in the overall space economy. *Acta Astronautica*, 219, 236–242.

Hodgson, G. (2002). Darwinism in economics: From analogy to ontology. *Journal of Evolutionary Economics*, 12, 259–281.

Hodgson, G. (2015). *Conceptualizing Capitalism: Institutions, Evolution, Future*. Chicago: University of Chicago Press.

Jaspers, K. (1948). The axial age of human history. *Commentary*, 6, 430.

Jones, C. and Tonetti, C. (2020). Nonrivalry and the economics of data. *American Economic Review*, 110(9), 2819–2858.

Kahn, D. (1967). *The Codebreakers: The Story of Secret Writing*. New York: Macmillan.

Kauffman, S. (2018). The evolution of economic webs. In P. W. Anderson, K. J. Arrow, & D. Pines (eds.), *The Economy as an Evolving Complex System*, pp. 125–146. Boca Raton, FL: CRC Press.

Kauffman, S. (1993). *The Origin of Order*. New York: Oxford University Press.

Kealey, T. and Ricketts, M. (2014). Modelling science as a contribution good. *Research Policy*, 43(6), 1014–1024.

Kirzner, I. (1973). *Competition and Entrepreneurship*. Chicago: University of Chicago Press.

Koppl, R., Cazzolla Gatti, R., Devereaux, A., et al. (2023). *Explaining Technology*. Cambridge: Cambridge University Press.

Kremer, M. (1993). Population growth and technological change: One million B.C to 1990. *Quarterly Journal of Economics*, 108, 681–716.

Kydland, F. and Prescott, E. (1982). Time to build and aggregate fluctuations. *Econometrica*, 50(6), 1345–1369.

Leeson, P. T. (2014). *Anarchy Unbound*. New York: Cambridge University Press.

Leiner, B., Cerf, V., Clark, D., et al. (2003). A brief history of the internet. *ACM SIGCOMM Computer Communication Review*, 39(5), 22–31.

Lessig, L. (2009). *Code: And Other Laws of Cyberspace*. New York: Basic Books.

Lloyd, S. (2009). Privacy and the quantum internet. *Scientific American*, 301(4), 80–85.

Lutomirski, A., Aaronson, S., Farhi, E., et al. (2009). Breaking and making quantum money: Toward a new quantum cryptographic protocol. *arXiv.org*.

Lv, Z., Lv, Z., Qiao, L., Kumar Singh, A., & Wang, Q. (2021). AI-empowered IoT security for smart cities. *ACM Transactions on Internet Technology*, 21(4), 1–21.

MacDonald, A. (2017). *The Long Space Age: The Economic Origins of Space Exploration from Colonial America to the Cold War*. New Haven: Yale University Press.

MacDonald, T. (2019). *The Political Economy of Non-territorial Exit*. Cheltenham: Edward Elgar.

Manin, Y. I. (1980). Vychislimoe i nevychislimoe (Computable and Uncomputable). Sov. radio.

Marchant, G. (2020). Governance of emerging technologies as a wicked problem. *Vanderbilt Law Review*, 73, 1861.

Marengo, A. (2024). Navigating the nexus of AI and IoT: A comprehensive review of data analytics and privacy paradigms. *Internet of Things*, 27-(101318), 1–22.

Mazzucato, M. (2021). *Mission Economy*. London: Penguin UK.

McCloskey, D. (2006). *The Bourgeois Virtues*. Chicago: University of Chicago Press.

McCloskey, D. (2016). *Bourgeois Equality*. Chicago: University of Chicago Press.

McCloskey, D. and Mingardi, A. (2020). *The Myth of the Entrepreneurial State*. Great Barrington, MA: American Institute for Economic Research.

Mill, J. S. (1859). *On Liberty*. London: John W. Parker and Son.

Miller, M. and Drexler, K. E. (1988). Markets and computation: Agoric open systems. In B. Huberman (ed.), *The Ecology of Computation*. Amsterdam: Elsevier.

Miller, M., Tulloh, W., and Shapiro, J. (2005). The structure of authority: Why security is not a separable concern. In P. Van Roy (ed.), *Multiparadigm Programming in Mozart/Oz* (Lecture Notes in Artificial Intelligence, Vol. 3389, pp. 2–20). Berlin: Springer-Verlag.

Mirowski, P. (2001). *Machine Dreams: Economics Becomes a Cyborg Science*. Cambridge: Cambridge University Press.

Mises, L. (1949). *Human Action. A Treatise on Economics*. New Haven, CT: Yale University Press.

Mohan, V. (2022). Automated market makers and decentralized exchanges: A DeFi primer. *Financial Innovation*, 8(20), 1–48.

Mokyr, J. (1990). *The Lever of Riches: Technological Creativity and Economic Progress*. New York: Oxford University Press.

Mokyr, J. (2016). *A Culture of Growth*. Princeton: Princeton University Press.

Moudoud, H., Cherkaoui, S., and Khoukhi, L. (2019). An IoT blockchain architecture using oracles and smart contracts. In *2019 IEEE 30th Annual International Symposium on Personal, Indoor and Mobile Radio Communications (PIMRC)*, pp. 1–6.

Murtazashvili, I., Murtazashvili, J., Weiss, M., and Madison, M. (2022). Blockchain networks as knowledge commons. *International Journal of the Commons*, 16(1), 108–119.

Nabben, K. (2023). Cryptoeconomics as governance: An intellectual history from "Crypto Anarchy" to "Cryptoeconomics". *Internet Histories: Digital Technology, Culture and Society*, 7(3), 1–23.

Nabben, K. and Zargham, M. (2022). Permissionlessness. *Internet Policy Review*, 11(2), 1–10.

Nakamoto, S. (2008). *Bitcoin: A Peer-to-Peer Electronic Cash System*.

Nelson, R. and Winter, S. (1982). *An Evolutionary Theory of Economic Change*. Cambridge, MA: Harvard University Press.

North, D. C. (1981). *Structure and Change in Economic History*. London: W. W. Norton & Co.

North, D. (1990). *Institutions, Institutional Change, and Economic Performance*. New York: Cambridge University Press.

North, D. (1991). Institutions. *Journal of Economic Perspectives*, 5(1): 97–112.

North, D. C. (1994). Economic performance through time. *The American Economic Review*, 84(3), 359–368.

North, D. (2005). *Understanding the Process of Economic Change*. Princeton: Princeton University Press.

North, D. and Thomas, R. (1973). *The Rise of the Western World*. New York: Cambridge University Press.

North, D., Wallis, J., and Weingast, B. (2009). *Violence and Social Orders*. New York: Cambridge University Press.

Ortman, S., Lobo, J., and Smith, M. (2020). Cities: Complexity, theory and history. *PloS One*, 15(12), e0243621.

Ostrom, E. (1990). *Governing the Commons*. Cambridge: Cambridge University Press.

Ostrom, E. (2005). *Understanding Institutional Diversity*. Princeton: Princeton University Press.

Pal, D. and Joshi, S. (2023). AI, IoT and robotics in smart farming: Current applications and future potentials. In *2023 International Conference on Sustainable Computing and Data Communication Systems*, pp. 1096–1101.

Plato (1927). *Charmides. Alcibiades I and II. Hipparchus. The Lovers. Theages. Minos. Epinomis: Charmides Alcibiades Hipparchus Lovers Theages Minos*

Epinomis. Translated by W. R. M. Lamb. 1st ed. Cambridge: Loeb Classical Library.

Potts, J. (2000). *The New Evolutionary Microeconomics*. Cheltenham: Edward Elgar.

Potts, J. (2010). Innovation by elimination: A proposal for negative policy experiments in the public sector. *Innovation*, 12(2), 238–248.

Potts, J. (2017). Institutions hold consumption on a leash: An evolutionary economic approach to the future of consumption. *Journal of Evolutionary Economics*, 27(2), 239–250.

Potts, J. (2019). *Innovation Commons*. Oxford: Oxford University Press.

Potts, J. (2023). Douglass north and the crypto-economy. *SSRN*.

Potts, J., Torrance, A., Harhoff, D., and von Hippel, E. (2024). Profiting from data commons: theory, evidence and strategy implications. *Strategy Science*, 9(1), 1–17.

Rennie, E. (2023). The CredSperiment: An ethnography of a contributions system. *SSRN*.

Rennie, E., Zargham, M., Tan, J., et al. (2022). Toward a participatory digital ethnography of blockchain governance. *Qualitative Inquiry*, 28(7), 837–847.

Rennie, E., & Potts, J. (2024). Contribution systems: A new theory of value. *SSRN*.

Richerson, P. and Boyd, R. (2005). *Not by Genes Alone*. Chicago: University of Chicago Press.

Rid, T. (2016). *Rise of the Machines: The Lost History of Cybernetics*. New York: W. W. Norton.

Rogaway, P. (2015). The moral character of cryptographic work (2015 IACR Distinguished Lecture) presented at Asiacrypt 2 December 2015, Auckland, New Zealand.

Rogers, E. (1962). *Diffusion of Innovations*. Illinois: Free Press of Glencoe.

Rogers, E., Singhal, A., and Quinlan, M. (2014). Diffusion of innovations. In D. W. Stacks and M. B. Salwen (eds.), *An Integrated Approach to Communication Theory and Research*, pp. 432–448. England: Routledge.

Rohde, P., Mohan, V., Davidson, S., et al. (2021). Quantum crypto-economics: Blockchain prediction markets for the evolution of quantum technology, *SSRN*.

Romer, P. (1986). Increasing returns and long-run growth. *Journal of Political Economy*, 94, 1002–1037.

Romer, P. M. (1990). Endogenous technological change. *Journal of Political Economy*, 98(5), S71–S102.

Rosenberg, N. (1982). *Inside the Black Box: Technology and Economics*. Cambridge: Cambridge University Press.

Roth, A. (1982). The economics of matching: Stability and incentives. *Mathematics of Operations Research*, 7(4), 617–628.

Sasson, E. B., Chiesa, A., Garman, C., Green, M., Miers, I., Tromer, E., & Virza, M. (2014, May). *Zerocash: Decentralized anonymous payments from bitcoin*. In *2014 IEEE Symposium on Security and Privacy* (pp. 459–474). IEEE: Piscataway, NJ.

Schrepel, T. (2024). The evolution of economies, technologies, and other institutions: Exploring W. Brian Arthur's insights. *Journal of Institutional Economics*, 20.

Schumpeter, J. (1939) *Business Cycles: A Theoretical, Historical and Statistical Analysis*, 1–15, 2 vols. New York: McGraw Hill.

Schumpeter, J. (1942). *Capitalism, Socialism and Democracy*. New York: Basic Books.

Scott, J. C. (1999). *Seeing Like a State: How Certain Schemes to Improve the Human Condition Have Failed*. New Haven, CT: Yale University Press.

Searle, J. (2005). What is an institution? *Journal of Institutional Economics*, 1(1), 1–22.

Shor, P. W. (1994). Algorithms for quantum computation: Discrete logarithms and factoring. In *Proceedings 35th Annual Symposium on Foundations of Computer Science*, pp. 124–34.

Simon, H. (1962). The architecture of complexity. *Proceedings of the American Philosophical Society*, 106(6), 467–482.

Simon, H. (1968). *The Sciences of the Artificial*. Cambridge, MA: MIT Press.

Singh, A., Sivangi, K., and Tentu, A. (2024). Machine learning and cryptanalysis: An In-depth exploration of current practices and future potential. *Journal of Computing Theories and Applications*, 1(3), 257–272.

Smith, A. W. (2024). Ecological institutions → Protocols to grow autonomous and convivial ecological actors. https://mirror.xyz/austinwadesmith.eth/tv9z1XXrtqQxDIxE8FygZ_W39NpkQJkVfrtjCtdbzA8.

Soete, L. and Freeman, C. (2012). *The Economics of Industrial Innovation*. London: Routledge.

Solow, R. M. (1956). A contribution to the theory of economic growth. *The Quarterly Journal of Economics*, 70(1), 65–94.

Srinivasan, B. (2022). *The Network State*.

Stallman, R. (2002). Free software, free society: Selected essays of Richard M. Stallman. Lulu.com.

Stigler, G. (1961). The economics of information. *Journal of Political Economy*, 69(3), 213–225.

Stigler, G. (1971). The theory of economic regulation. *Bell Journal of Economics and Management Science*, 2(1), 3–21.

Stringham, E. (2015). *Private Governance*. Oxford: Oxford University Press.

Summers, L. (2016). The age of secular stagnation: What it is and what to do about it. *Foreign Affairs*, 95(2), 2–9.

Teece, D. (2012). Next-generation competition: New concepts for understanding how innovation shapes competition and policy in the digital economy. *Journal of Law, Economics and Policy*, 9(1), 97–118.

Teece, D. (2018). Profiting from innovation in the digital economy: Enabling technologies, standards, and licensing models in the wireless world. *Research Policy*, 47(8), 1367–1387.

Thierer, A. (2016). *Permissionless Innovation*. Arlington, VA: Mercatus Center at George Mason University.

Tozzi, C. (2017). *For Fun and Profit: A History of the Free and Open Source Software Revolution*. Cambridge, MA: MIT Press.

Turing, A. (1950). Computing machinery and intelligence. *Mind*, LIX(236), 433–460.

Turner, F. (2006). *From Counterculture to Cyberculture: Stewart Brand, the Whole Earth Network, and the Rise of Digital Utopianism*. Chicago: University of Chicago Press.

Vance, A. (2023). *When the Heavens Went on Sale*. New York: Ecco.

von Hippel, E. (2016). *Free Innovation*. Cambridge, MA: MIT Press.

Von Neumann, J. (1945). A model of general economic equilibrium. *Review of Economic Studies*, 13, 1–9.

Wang, R., Zhang, S., Yang, B. et al. (2024). Enabling data sharing through data trusts in LEO satellite internet. *IEEE Wireless Communications*, 31(1), 70–76.

Warsh, D. (2006). *Knowledge and the Wealth of Nations*. New York: W.W. Norton.

Waters-Lynch, J., Allen, D. W. E., Potts, J., and Berg, C. (2024). Managing Generative AI in Firms: The Theory of Shadow User Innovation. *SSRN*.

Weinzierl, M. (2018). Space, the final economic frontier. *Journal of Economic Perspectives*, 32(2), 173–192.

Weinzierl, M. (2023). Expanding economic activity in space may offer a solution to secular stagnation. *PNAS*, 120, 43.

Weitzman, M. (1998). Recombinant growth. *Quarterly Journal of Economics*, 113(2), 331–360.

Weyl, E., Ohlhaver, P., and Buterin, V. (2022). Decentralized society: Finding web3's soul. *SSRN 4105763*.

Wiesner, S. (1983). Conjugate coding. *SIGACT News*, 15(1), 78–88.

Williamson, O. (2000). The new institutional economics: Taking stock, looking ahead. *Journal of Economic Literature*, 38(3), 595–615.

Wootters, W. and Zurek, W. (1982). A single quantum cannot be cloned. *Nature*, 299(5886), 802–803.

Xu, J., Perez, D., Feng, Y., & Livshits, B. (2023). Auto. gov: Learning-based on-chain governance for decentralized finance (defi). *arXiv preprint,* arXiv:2302.09551.

Zhandry, M. (2021). Quantum lightning never strikes the same state Twice. Or: Quantum money from cryptographic assumptions. *Journal of Cryptology*, 34(6), 1–62.

Zhang, K., Song, X., Zhang, C., & Yu, S. (2022). Challenges and future directions of secure federated learning: A survey. *Frontiers of Computer Science*, 16(5), 165817.

Ziman, J. (ed.) (2000). *Technological Innovation as an Evolutionary Process*. New York: Cambridge University Press.

Cambridge Elements

Evolutionary Economics

John Foster
University of Queensland

John Foster is Emeritus Professor of Economics and former Head of the School of Economics at the University of Queensland, Brisbane. He is Fellow of the Academy of Social Science in Australia, Life member of Clare Hall College, Cambridge and Past President of the International J.A. Schumpeter Society.

Jason Potts
RMIT University

Jason Potts is Professor of Economics at RMIT University, Melbourne. He is also an Adjunct Fellow at the Institute of Public Affairs. His research interests include technological change, economics of innovation, and economics of cities. He was the winner of the 2000 International Joseph A. Schumpeter Prize and has published over 60 articles and six books.

Isabel Almudi
University of Zaragoza

Isabel Almudi is Professor of Economics at the University of Zaragoza, Spain, where she also belongs to the Instituto de Biocomputación y Física de Sistemas Complejos. She has been Visiting Fellow at the European University Institute, Columbia University and RMIT University. Her research fields are evolutionary economics, innovation studies, environmental economics and dynamic systems.

Francisco Fatas-Villafranca
University of Zaragoza

Francisco Fatas-Villafranca is Professor of Economics at the University of Zaragoza, Spain. He has been Visiting Scholar at Columbia University and Visiting Researcher at the University of Manchester. His research focuses on economic theory and quantitative methods in the social sciences, with special interest in evolutionary economics.

David A. Harper
New York University

David A. Harper is Clinical Professor of Economics and Co-Director of the Program on the Foundations of the Market Economy at New York University. His research interests span institutional economics, Austrian economics and evolutionary economics. He has written two books and has published extensively in academic journals. He was formerly Chief Analyst and Manager at the New Zealand Treasury.

About the Series

Cambridge Elements of Evolutionary Economics provides authoritative and up-to-date reviews of core topics and recent developments in the field. It includes state-of-the-art contributions on all areas in the field. The series is broadly concerned with questions of dynamics and change, with a particular focus on processes of entrepreneurship and innovation, industrial and institutional dynamics, and on patterns of economic growth and development.

Cambridge Elements

Evolutionary Economics

Elements in the Series

A Reconsideration of the Theory of Non-Linear Scale Effects: The Sources of Varying Returns to, and Economics of, Scale
Richard G. Lipsey

Evolutionary Economics: Its Nature and Future
Geoffrey M. Hodgson

Coevolution in Economic Systems
Isabel Almudi and Francisco Fatas-Villafranca

Industrial Policy: The Coevolution of Public and Private Sources of Finance for Important Emerging and Evolving Technologies
Kenneth I. Carlaw and Richard G. Lipsey

Explaining Technology
Roger Koppl, Roberto Cazzolla Gatti, Abigail Devereaux, Brian D. Fath, James Herriot, Wim Hordijk, Stuart Kauffman, Robert E. Ulanowicz and Sergi Valverde

Evolutionary Games and the Replicator Dynamics
Saul Mendoza-Palacios and Onésimo Hernández-Lerma

The Dynamic Metacapabilities Framework: Introducing Quantum Management and the Informational View of the Firm
Harold Paredes-Frigolett and Andreas Pyka

Entrepreneurship and Evolutionary Economics
Per L. Bylund

Agent-Based Macroeconomics: The Schumpeter Meeting Keynes Models
Giovanni Dosi and Andrea Roventini

Evolutionary Price Theory
Harry Bloch

Institutional Acceleration: The Consequences of Technological Change in a Digital Economy
Darcy W. E. Allen, Chris Berg and Jason Potts

A full series listing is available at: www.cambridge.org/EEVE

For EU product safety concerns, contact us at Calle de José Abascal, 56–1°, 28003 Madrid, Spain or eugpsr@cambridge.org.

www.ingramcontent.com/pod-product-compliance
Lightning Source LLC
LaVergne TN
LVHW020350260326
834688LV00045B/1641